EYE OF THE TIGER

EYE OF THE TIGER

Memoir of a United States Marine,
Third Force Recon Company, Vietnam

John Edmund Delezen

McFarland & Company, Inc., Publishers
Jefferson, North Carolina, and London

Library of Congress Online catalog Data

Delezen, John Edmund, 1947–
    Eye of the tiger : memoir of a United States Marine,
Third Force Recon Company, Vietnam / John Edmund
Delezen.
        p.   cm.
    Includes bibliographical references and index.

    ISBN-13: 978-0-7864-1656-1
    (softcover : 50# alkaline paper) ∞

    1. Delezen, John Edmund, 1947–   2. United States.
Marine Corps. Force Reconaissance Company, 3rd—History.
3. Vietnamese Conflict, 1961–1975—Personal narratives,
American.   4. Vietnamese Conflict, 1961–1975—Regimental
histories–United States.   I. Title.
DS559.5.D45   2003
959.704'342B—dc21   2003013004

British Library cataloguing data are available

Cover illustration and design by Kace Montgomery,
    Iron Block Design

Manufactured in the United States of America

McFarland & Company, Inc., Publishers
*   Box 611, Jefferson, North Carolina 28640*
    www.mcfarlandpub.com

Le Dédicace

This effort is for those that felt the effects of the far away "ambush war" ... it is for those that were once my enemy and now call me friend and brother. It is for my lost comrades whose souls will forever wander through the fragrant grottos of the Truong Son. It is for the men and women that experienced the madness and returned to America only to find themselves unwelcomed strangers in an ungrateful land. It is for the maimed and it is for those that are visited each night by old familiar demons. It is for our South Vietnamese allies, those that were deserted by the jaded nation that once called them "friend." It is for the oppressed who perished in the "re-education" camps and for the wretched who died at sea...

Merci Beaucoup
(Acknowledgments)

Special acknowledgments must go to so many—too many to list. So many have helped me through this effort, not only by providing an accurate and precise presentation of events, but with help in dealing with the emotional stress that accompanies the reemergence of experiences that were once locked away in "sealed boxes" by a young "bush Marine." It was not my plan to write a book; I sat down to write a brief outline of Vietnamese history for a friend and could not stop ... it gushed from me in torrents.

I want to offer my sincere thanks to the following: my wife Kelly, *je t'aime*; Richard Delezen, for listening to my insane ravings when no one else would; Ron Kittren (the Sergeant in *The Trail* and *The Border*), for many years of cherished friendship; Bill Whittemore (the PFC in *The Border*), who left us too early and when he left, life lost much of its color; Art Loder ("the point" in *Ca Lu* and in *Hunger*), for his kind help and treasured friendship; Billy Andress (the Team Leader in *The Rain* and *The River*), always there, he is a true friend and brother; Frank DeMoss (the Team Leader in *Hunger, The Gift* and *Da Nang*); Dennis Spear, gone but not forgotten; Bill Floyd (the Major) for his encouragement and help, not just with this book but for too many other things to list; Nevitt D.

Davis, the bravest person that I have ever known (*repos dans la paix, mon ami*); Patrick Lucanio, Ph.D., for too much help to list; Marion Sturkey (author of *Bonnie Sue: A Marine Helicopter Squadron in Vietnam*) for guidance and encouragement; George "Digger" O'Dell, for assistance, concern and support; Leland Robinson, a true friend and fellow bush Marine; an old friend, Patrick Martin, Ph.D., for much needed support; Mike Mullen, Ph.D. (the pilot of ET-3: *The Trail*)—I owe my life to his skills as an aviator; Richard Herberg (*The Trail*), who flew the rescue helicopter and was awarded the DFC; and Dave Ellis (*The Trail*), port gunner on the rescue helicopter. Thanks are also due to the many Vietnamese scholars that have helped me with difficult translations, my adopted family and friends in Vietnam, the poet Tran Dien, my good friends Phuoc Loc and Tong Phuoc Quang, and of course, Brian Clery (the free lance reporter from *Hunger*), wherever you are.

Contents

Contents

Military History of John Edmund Delezen

John Edmund Delezen entered the U.S. Marine Corps in August 1965 and reported for basic training at Parris Island, South Carolina. After infantry training at Camp Geiger, North Carolina, he volunteered in November 1965 for the Third Force Recon Company that was forming there.

More training followed: U.S. Army Airborne School at Fort Benning, Georgia, in December 1965; rubber boat and submarine training in Vieques, Puerto Rico, in February 1966; and Special Forces Jungle Warfare School in the Panama Canal Zone, also in February. In the summer of 1966, the Third Force Recon relocated to California. Delezen attended the U.S. Navy Underwater Swimmers Course at San Diego in January 1967.

Three months later, in March, he was assigned to the advance part and left San Diego for Vietnam aboard the USS *Catamount* (LSD-17). The party arrived at Dong Ha, Republic of Vietnam, in April and were joined by the rest of the unit within days. They were assigned to perform reconnaissance work along the Demilitarized Zone and Laotian border.

Malaria struck Delezen in November 1967. He was sent to the USS *Repose* and also spent time in hospitals in Da Nang and Phu

Bai. He received two wounds, was shot down in a helicopter and had another bout with malaria before being honorably discharged. In February 1968 he was wounded by a grenade north of Mutters Ridge. In late summer he was wounded by rifle fire west of Khe Sanh, and in August he was shot down in a CH-46 helicopter during an insertion into the Da Krong Valley. He was sent home because of malaria in December 1968 and honorably discharged in May 1969.

His decorations and awards include Purple Heart with Star, Navy Commendation Medal with V, Vietnamese Cross of Gallantry, Combat Action Ribbon, Good Conduct, Navy Unit Citation, Presidential Unit Citation, Navy-Marine Unit Commendation, National Defense, Vietnam Civic Action with Palm, Vietnam Campaign with 5 Stars, Vietnam Service, Expert Rifle Badge, Pistol Sharpshooter Badge, Navy-Marine Parachute Wings, U.S. Army Parachute Wings, U.S. Navy Underwater Swimmers Badge, Vietnamese Parachute Wings, U.S. Army Jungle Expert Award, and High School Equivalency (GED) in 1966.

In war, then,
Let your great object be victory,
not lengthy campaigns.

Sun Tzu

1

Ho Mang Chua

It is the Annam Cordillera that I am facing. On the old French maps it is called the Chaîne Annamitique, but to the Vietnamese it is the Truong Son, a holy place that has kept invaders at bay for centuries. The ancient mountain range thrusts abruptly up from the fringe of fertile coastal plain and into the low clouds; steep shards of gray and black stone that form the peaks are hidden beneath a thick blanket of dark green rain forest. From a distance the encasement of jungle resembles a rumpled, green velvet cloak. It is a very dark green that is sometimes accented by the blazing colors of wild orchids that grow high in the treetops. Along the razor edged ridges that connect the higher peaks, powerful eagles glide; occasionally they dive into the thick canopy for an unsuspecting monkey or snake. We are told that there are as many as three canopies, layers of thick vegetation blocking the sun from the ones below. The first canopy is not very high from the rain forest floor and if you look up through the entangled vines and branches, you may see the second. The third canopy is seldom seen, though we can hear the monkeys and birds that live high in the towering teak and mahogany trees. The steamy ground is always damp and is covered with a thick layer of rotting leaves; hordes of glistening leeches live in the musty dampness and in the canopy above, their voracious hunger is insatiable. Huge butterflies with wings emblazoned in dazzling colors and intricate patterns dwarf the smaller

1

birds; their iridescent wings flash as tiny golden streams of atypical sunlight filter through the triple canopy. There is seldom an opening in the canopy for the searing sun to enter this humid, mushroomed world of dark shadows. Occasionally a bomb will detonate in the high canopy and create the ragged entry that will allow a lone, bright serpentine pillar of blinding sunlight to pass through to the thick peat; the dark floor that has never known unfiltered sunlight soon fills with huge stands of thick, golden bamboo. The grotto never stops growing. It is early summer 1967; this is the Vietnam that I know.

> *O divine art of subtlety and secrecy!*
> *Through you we learn to be invisible,*
> *Through you inaudible;*
> *And hence we can hold the enemy's*
> *fate in our hands.*
>
> Sun Tzu

We are Marine Recon, often called the "eyes and ears" of the Third Marine Division. We are sent into the Truong Son to locate hidden, illusive enemy units; here we learn the discipline of the bush as we discover and travel the paths of knowledge blazed by ancient Confucian warriors. We hone our lethal craft as we learn to live and survive under the thick canopy, becoming a part of the bush, always aware, always searching, and always moving with deadly stealth. Our creed, "Swift, Silent, and Deadly," means little to the troops in the rear areas, merely shallow words; but here in these steaming, dark, jungle-choked mountains, we become the words. We are those who will remain obscure long after America loses interest in our war; we will never seek nor receive the recognition that will be given to other units. It is because we are Marines and we know that we are no better than any of our Marine brothers. Our unit merely supports the essence of the Corps, which is the rifle battalion. We wear no unit patches because the Marine Corps will not tolerate individualism; our small unit is but part of a team, nothing more, and we want nothing more. Due to the Spartan ideology that is part of being a Marine, few individual decorations are awarded; what many consider valor, we merely consider our duty. We are a band of brothers, we are comrades, and we are family; long after America has discarded us we will continue to seek counsel with one another. We will maintain our family ties long after we depart the Annam Cordillera; for many of us it will be the only true family that we will ever know.

We live with fear and he becomes our ally. With his constant presence, he sharpens our awareness with the icy blasts of adrenaline that flow from deep within us, perhaps from a source long forgotten in the progression of evolution; he is the catalyst that has transformed us into a "hunting pack." Hearing, smell, taste, and sight are amplified under the canopy and we possess the wild, blazing white eyes of both predator and prey. They are wide, scanning eyes that continuously search, constantly penetrate, and are permanently frozen into the perpetual strain that comes from months of staring painfully into thick masses of vine-choked jungle.

Under the canopy we hunt our adversary, the North Vietnamese soldier. To us he is the "gook," the "dink"; he is neither the "Charlie" nor the "VC" that is so popular among the rear area troops. They are not words spawned by racial motives but rather the words that command respect and generate fear; with the passing of our youth and the emergence of a deeply repressed sensitivity, some of us will one day unearth a terrible shame in having once used them.

In the heat and rain of the Truong Son, the North Vietnamese soldier is our prey and we are his. We live together under the thick canopy, each searching for the other; the same leeches and mosquitoes that feed on our blood feed on his blood. He hears the same tigers and coal black leopards that prowl so close at night; he sees the same piercing eyes that stare from the black void as dim rays of distant illumination rounds summon fire from the huge cats like yellow diamonds. Our enemy was sent into the Annam Mountains to kill us; to accomplish this he must also learn to hunt and learn to survive here.

Our small teams prowl these deadly mountain grottos seeking an enemy that we seldom see. We are brought here by helicopter and inserted into this strange world; if there is no opening in the canopy for the helicopter to penetrate, jet fighters will blast a hole with high explosive bombs. Other times, the helicopter will hover above the trees as we rappel through the canopy, snaking our way down a doubled nylon rope to the floor of the jungle. Often I wonder, are those we hunt our true enemy? Perhaps it is the bush that is the enemy or perhaps it is those who have sent us into this lush and tranquil garden of orchids. Like our enemy, we are sent here by an older generation to defend a political policy that few of us understand. Neither the "gook" nor the "grunt" have an interest in policy and only understand survival; yet both are patriots that have met here in the shadows of the Truong Son to fight and perhaps leave their wandering souls. We are young and our enemy is young, we share so much, so many hardships; are we brothers? Are we killing our brothers? If so, which is Cain and which is Abel, which of us are Yin and which of us Yang? Who is the innocent and who is the guilty and which of us is the victim? Perhaps the victim is our youth.

Time has neither beginning nor end here and though the lowlands give the Vietnamese rice, their staple, it is the highlands that give the people their legends, art and religion. Fearing the dark shadows of the rain forest, most Vietnamese will not venture into the Truong Son, where countless ages have deposited the restless, wandering souls of those who will never reach Nirvana.

In the lowlands the lord of the rice is Ho Mang, the Cobra. He is protector of the crop, fending off the hordes of rats that attack the lush, green, flooded paddies. Though feared, the farmers recognize his importance and know Ho Mang as a friend and as a brother; but in the thick, canopied grottos and high grassy plateaus of the Truong Son it is Ho Mang Chua that is lord. He is the King Cobra, the Holy Snake, a brother to none, a God to all; a fleeting giant phantom that jealously protects his grotto. Always searching for the intruder, he is the reincarnate of ancient royalty and all others willingly pay homage. Neither Con Ho, the tiger, nor Con Voi, the elephant, threaten him; he allows their presence in his kingdom and though they are royalty, neither will challenge Ho Mang Chua for dominance, for he is the Truong Son ... he is Vietnam ... he is all.

4

Ho Mang near Nui Con Thien.

Soon we will encounter the lord of the Truong Son and like those that came before us, upon entering into his realm, we must offer reverence. He watches us, as does Con Ho, from deep within the mystery of drifting shadows he remains invisible, yet near; he will be here when our bones are forgotten dust and our tattered, insignificant page of history has been lost in a myriad of time—for he is eternal. Ancient legends state that his droppings are the seeds that have sent the vivid streams of orchids streaking through the canopy, seeking the sun; he has no enemy, the Truong Son is his garden, his verdant monarchy.

2

Nui Con Thien

To the Marines and North Vietnamese that battle along the Demilitarized Zone, Nui Con Thien is the high ground, the prize. It sits alone in the vast expanse of abandoned French plantations that have been transformed from lush, tranquil gardens into the blasted, scorched hell of ambush-laden hedgerows, ravines, and cart trails. Though Nui Con Thien barely rises a mere 158 meters, it dominates the terrain for at least four kilometers in any direction; the Marines exploit this feature and have established a small outpost on and around the little barren hill. Encircled concentrically with massive amounts of barbed and razor wire, the tiny hill serves as an observation post and a radio relay, and is the support center for the Marine rifle companies that maneuver through the area. Our overextended and undermanned division has been ordered to conduct search-and-destroy operations along the Demilitarized Zone (DMZ), though Marine leaders have rejected this strategy, recognizing it as a useless way to fight an illusive enemy that enjoys the sanctuary north of the DMZ. From across the Ben Hai River, just five kilometers to the northwest and eight kilometers to the north, enemy artillery units pound Con Thien around the clock with long- and short-range mortars, howitzers, recoilless rifles, and rockets. From the vantage point of our enemy, the outpost is an exposed target; it is clearly visible from North Vietnam, requiring no forward observer to adjust the deadly barrages. The fifteen kilometers that stretch eastward from Con Thien to her sister outpost at Gio Linh have been scraped clear by bulldozers; it is hoped that the cleared strip will prevent infiltration by large enemy units. To the politicians it is known as the "McNamara Barrier," but to the grunts that will patrol and defend this cleared hell, it is simply the "Trace"; it is a concept that reeks of stagnation, incompetence and death.

Only four kilometers to the west of the outpost, the terrain changes abruptly. The long neglected and ravaged plantations suddenly meet the green foothills of the Truong Son that are choked with tall elephant grass; hidden in the tall grass are deep, treacherous ravines that offer concealment for maneuvering enemy units. The contrast is vivid, the torn and mauled scrub of the overgrown plantations seems to cry out for mercy; I am made to wonder how much more suffering this once beautiful plot of earth can endure. Each day, sorties of jet fighters attack with loads of napalm; orange-black walls of fire roll and churn across the land sucking the oxygen from all life forms while deafening blasts from white-hot afterburners seem to add to the ruthless heat of the blistering sun. The rich, pungent soil is plowed and turned as bombs, artillery, mortars and rockets burrow and blast deep craters into the tortured red earth. As the hidden guns and rocket launchers of our enemy fire at the tiny outpost from their haven in North Vietnam, barrages answer them from obscure firebases that are scattered across this northernmost part of South Vietnam. Observation aircraft prowl the area searching for the telltale muzzle flashes of the enemy artillery and each night "Spooky" arrives spitting laser-like streams of brilliant orange tracers into the hell below. From the South China Sea, destroyers and cruisers add to the carnage with salvoes of naval gunfire. The earth that spans the distance from Con Thien to her sister outpost to the east at Gio Linh has been plowed and churned from the onslaught for so long that it now resembles the surface of the moon. Though so much carnage has been delivered here, miraculously, the trees and brush continue to grow; often found are ravaged and splintered remnants of the huge rubber tree groves that once blanketed the area. The trunks of the trees are streaked with streams of thick, white liquid that flow from the deep wounds inflicted by shell fragments and jacketed bullets. Once this white

7

liquid was the wealth of Indochina, much more important than the café and opium grown on the high plateaus. Without the loving care of the planter that once nurtured them, the trees now bleed into the ravaged soil. The planter, forced from the land by the expanding madness, fled to France, leaving the groves to fend for themselves. The beauty, tranquility and peace that once nurtured the lush trees have been ripped from the earth and replaced by terror, pain and suffering. Now the trees that once were the focus of dreams and hopes have become abandoned, childlike orphans; the strong limbs that once were covered with lush fragrant greenery are now shattered, twisted, and charred ... reaching toward heaven ... as if begging for mercy and salvation.

The plantations that surround the little isolated hill once provided a hope of economic prosperity. The French colonial planters cultivated the rich, red earth and with the help of an endless supply of cheap coolie labor, a number of bountiful plantations were established. The twenty-five kilometers of rolling scrubland that traverse this section of Vietnam, from the Annam Cordillera to the South China Sea, has long been the path of Con Bao, the super-typhoon; the storms often sweep unopposed across this low land, devastating all that challenges the fierce wind and rain. The more fortunate planters, those that moved into the high plateaus of the Truong Son, were blessed with protection from the frequent storms and accumulated fortunes while growing the rich café that became a staple of France. Later, as Café Society emerged from the despair of the Great War, a "lost generation" found solace in the sidewalk fellowship where fresh ideas were discovered and shared. Whether the view was along the *Quai de Passy* in Paris where ideas influenced by Dada flourished or along the *Rue Catinate* in Saigon where plans of revolution and independence were discussed, the superior café from the high plateaus of the Annam Cordillera was in demand.

Those that chose to remain in the lowland to seek their fortune in rubber realized that the sheltered land far to the south was less prone to the onslaught of typhoons. There the vast coastal plain becomes much broader as the mountains gradually lose their magnificence, melting into the flat, fertile soil of what was once the Khmer Kingdom. Many relocated their rubber groves and were blessed

8

with prosperity. A defiant few remained in the shadows of Nui Con Thien to battle the wrath of nature and experiment with various crops more suited to the rage of Con Bao. French priests and nuns that had established schools, clinics, orphanages and missions throughout the area also remained. Though the earth that surrounds the Con Thien area was very rich, and there were small shipping ports nearby on the Ben Hai and the Cua Viet Rivers, as well as the railroad that snaked its way the full length of Vietnam, it was a gamble for planters to invest so much time and effort in the typhoon path. Although a number of planters enjoyed prosperity, Con Thien would never become the dynamic agricultural center enjoyed by so much of Vietnam.

> *There will be formed a Legion*
> *Composed of Foreigners*
> *This Legion will take the name of*
> *Foreign Legion.*
>
> Louis-Phillippe, King of the French
> 9 March 1831

The Marines have been told, without careful thought, that Nui Con Thien is translated into "The Hill of Angels." It is a very romantic name, conjuring thoughts of a lonely, isolated French mission, protected by a few brave Legionnaires. In fact, the French troops did build and defend a fortification on the crest of the bare hill. The well built, steel reinforced fortifications were the foundation for the French strategy that placed very small units of troops in concrete bunkers to protect isolated infrastructure, strong points, and of course the representatives of the politically powerful Church. These brave units often repelled massive Viet Minh attacks while priests and nuns huddled with frightened orphans. As prayers of forgiveness were sent toward the oncoming enemy, smoking Legionnaire machine guns and mortars cut through the human wave assaults like blades through wheat. It was *Beau Geste*, it was romance, and from these lonely outposts was heard the defiant chorus of "Le Boudin," the marching song that is as old as the Legion itself. Their defiance thrust as much into the cold and uncaring face of France

9

May 1967. The author at Con Thien. Our 8-man "Stingray" team prepares to move west into the DMZ. Within hours we will be in heavy contact with a reinforced NVA company.

as into the face of the Viet Minh, their loyalty reserved only for the *Legion Etrangere*. French paratroops and infantry, fresh from the bitter cold of Korea, joined the Legionnaires and their *Indochine* allies; many fought to the death to defend the investments of the French colonial elite. It was perhaps France's finest hour—but few would ever know or care about such loyalty. And while French blood soaked deep into the Mandarin Road, the precious time was bought that would allow the accumulated wealth of Indochina to be transferred to the sanctuary of Swiss banks.

In the end France would abandon the colony and her men; of those captured, few would survive the long marches to the death camps along the Chinese border. Only the concrete bunkers would remain as testament to the futility of a careless strategy created by incompetent French politicians. And like the French, a jaded America will also abandon her friends, her ideals, as well as her sons, and in her haste to flee she will leave her virtue and her honor behind. The blood of another lost generation, her blood, will forever stain the lonely, damp, shell-scarred bunkers.

Though it is a beautiful name, "Hill of Angels" is not an accurate translation. Hardly any names of cities, rivers or mountains in Vietnam are unadulterated. Many are proper names that cannot be translated, others are ancient Chinese and Cham names that, having acquired Vietnamese font, were spelled the way they sounded. Along the borders Lao and Khmer names add to the confusion and isolated French names are also thrown in for good measure. The origins of many names were forgotten centuries ago; an excellent example is the *Song Cuu Long*, which translated from ancient Chinese means River of Nine Dragons, or arguably, River of Nine Serpents; to westerners it is the Me Kong River. Most Vietnamese have no interest in exploring the mysterious names, considering them to be something else that is just accepted and never questioned. The name Nui Con Thien has been offered to various scholars throughout Vietnam and each has returned a different theory as to the true meaning; most seem certain that the correct name is "The Angel." The name in its present form is not plural. In order for the name to translate into "Angel Hill," the Vietnamese name would have to be "Nui Con Thien-than." Nui Con translates into small mountain or hill; Thien-than, angel or the angel. Thien alone is incomplete and has no meaning and without the complete name it cannot be accurately translated. I want to believe the name to be "the Angel"; perhaps in haste to prepare the map of the region, a small significant piece of the label was omitted. Perhaps the little hill received the name as a term of endearment; standing alone in the low scrubland, perhaps it was seen as a watchful angel. The small, gently sloping hill may have been a place of prayer in more peaceful times. Perhaps Easter Mass was an annual event on the little hill, as colonials dressed in mail-ordered French fashions climbed the gentle slope to pray for a mild typhoon season while the orange-yellow sun rose from the sapphire blue of the South China Sea. Or perhaps it was named when it became a haven for the priests and nuns that sought sanctuary within the perimeter of the Legionnaires' barbed wire.

Though the incomplete name cannot be correctly translated, and the origin remains a mystery, it is perhaps best left undisturbed. As with most mysteries, the search could travel on and on, always in a great circle, until the path returns to the very spot that the search was launched. And when the truth is revealed and the origin known, there is always the name of the next mountain, village or river, and the next. Though the name remains wrapped in ambiguity, the blood that soaked into the cauldron has replaced the ancient name with another that is deeply etched into enduring lore and legend; to the Marines and South Vietnamese that defended this gentle rise, it will always be known as "The Hill of Angels."

The short distance that traverses the scrubland from the South China Sea to the foothills of the Annam Cordillera has known barriers other than the Trace. At the dawn of the fifteenth century, China once again invaded Vietnam. Having thrown off the yoke of the Mongols, the Ming dynasty attacked the Vietnamese in force to avenge the failed occupations of the past. After two decades of fierce war, the guerilla fighter Le Loi drove out the Ming. Immediately he occupied the throne of Vietnam, and from Ha Noi the Le Dynasty ruled all of the still expanding country.

In 1620, the governor of Hue, Nguyen Hoang, revolted against the Le Dynasty. He declared the land south of what is now the Ben Hai River to be an independent kingdom ruled by the Nguyen family. Bloody battles were fought along the eastern expanses of the border, as elephant armies clad in opulence and armor clashed around Nui Con Thien and Gio Linh. The weaker Nguyen army employed guerilla tactics, learned from Le Loi, against the stronger Le forces. While holding the Le at bay, the Nguyen constructed a series of walls, twenty-five feet in height, the longest of these traversed the twelve miles from the South China Sea to the foothills of the Annam Cordillera; no doubt, the wall incorporated the high ground of Nui Con Thien and Gio Linh. The powerful Le elephant

Opposite: Standing in front of our "hooch," Art Loder waits to board a CH-46 helicopter that will insert our team somewhere in the mountains. The lack of weather and shrapnel damage to the hooch, as well as the condition of Art's boots reveal that our unit has recently arrived in Vietnam (courtesy of Arthur Loder).

13

army was unable to destroy the Nguyen defenses and returned to the north. The border, established at the Ben Hai River, would separate the two countries until the Tay son Rebellion some one hundred years later.

And now, we have also come to this place to search for the ever-present enemy. Marine infantry and recon units will be bled dearly in the scorched plantations through the summer and fall; what the North Vietnamese leave of us will be sucked dry by the inferno of the ruthless sun. Con Thien is searing heat in spring and summer and it is a rain-swept sea of mud in fall and winter. Always, the stench of bloated, unburied enemy dead fills the void once occupied by fragrant mimosa, frangipani and mango flowers. There is never a pause from the madness; here in the shadow of the Hill of Angels there is only the promise of torture, death and decay.

3

The Dark

From our forward patrol base at Dong Ha, our team is trucked up to Con Thien. Recon inserts into the DMZ area by helicopter have been stopped. Now we must move overland from the outpost to reach our designated RZ (reconnaissance zone). We are to patrol a six square kilometer area that is some four and one half kilometers west of Con Thien; this area lies within the DMZ. To the grunts and recon teams, the area is called the "four-nineties"; the name has been attached due to four contour intervals on the map that are each labeled ninety meters in altitude and form a rectangle. Just to the south of this rectangle sits hill 174, the Devil lives there. The four-nineties sprawl before the Devil; they are his whores. The entire area is fortified with bunkers and tunnels. Anti-aircraft positions of 12.7mm and 37mm are concealed in the many deep ravines. Recently, a CH-46 was lost there during a recon insertion; the helicopter, *Echo Papa-158*, carrying its four-man aircrew and a seven-man recon team, suddenly inverted and burst into flames as it approached the designated insertion LZ (landing zone). We have been told little else. An effort to recover the bodies was met with heavy resistance from a massive, dug-in enemy force.

The move to our patrol area will take us across at least three kilometers of overgrown plantations to an area labeled on our maps as the Agricultural Development Center. From there it will be difficult to move, as the terrain changes abruptly from plantation to jungle ravines and thick elephant grass. It is very possible that at this instant our assigned RZ is perchance the most dangerous place in all of Vietnam.

Turning north from Route 9, our group of two trucks and one radio jeep crosses the wooden bridge at Cam Lo and follows the all-too-familiar dirt road to Con Thien; it is a road that we hate and fear. Our tiny convoy is enveloped in a thick cloud of red dust that chokes us. A shirtless gunner mans the .50-caliber machine gun turret that is mounted above and opposite the driver; the red dust has mixed with sweat and is running down his bare chest and arms like streams of blood. The heat is almost intolerable, red, muddy sweat pours from each of us; it flows in streams that are constantly replenished by long fetid drinks from plastic canteens. We pass through the C-2 firebase that is still under construction; the fortified positions of sandbagged bunkers that surround the new base are encircled by stacks of new concertina that shimmer in the fierce sun. To our left, west of the dry, eroded road, a platoon of Marines is sweeping north behind a slow moving tank. As the tank pivots and lunges, steel treads rip into the dry scrub, creating a monstrous cloud of dust that engulfs the following grunts; to prevent the dust from entering their lungs, most have tied shirts and empty bandoliers across their faces as makeshift filters. The dust from the tank drifts into our path and mixes into the red cloud that already engulfs us. The result is a churning red void that briefly blocks the sun; it turns the world into an orange tinted vacuum that threatens to suffocate both trucks and Marines. Above, the sun is uncompromising; it offers no compassion. I glance up and search painfully for our searing host, but there is no single source, the entire sky is filled with the yellow-white blistering inferno. There is no mountain canopy here; the blast furnace heat is all consuming. The summer hell of the eastern DMZ is as much the enemy to us as those that we are sent to locate and destroy.

The drivers take us to within a few hundred meters of the outpost. It is too dangerous to take the trucks closer; all vehicles, no matter their importance, offer an excellent target for hidden enemy forward observers that continuously watch for opportunities such as this. As each man jumps from the truck to the ground, a powdery cloud of red is released from his clothing. The dust enhances the heat, which now seems alive; we are already going to the canteens that must last for an unknown number of days. There is very little clean water to be found across the torn and ravaged plantations; we will need to drink water constantly as we move. When our clean water is gone, we will fill the canteens with stagnant slime from the floor of bomb craters.

Forming a column, we move up the hot road toward the barbed wire perimeter; from ahead, we can hear the blasts from enemy mortars that are lobbed indiscriminately into the tiny outpost searching for prey. As we near the necklace of concertina wire that surrounds the base, we come across a group of Marines that man a 60mm mortar. They are typical Marine grunts—skinny, filthy and ragged; we are invited to share the holes that they have dug. We are relieved that we will not have to go inside of the wire, which is the "bull's-eye" for the many rockets, mortars and artillery rounds that chew and claw at the hill each day and night. It is much safer outside the wire, at least until dark approaches. The team leader drops his pack and, accompanied by the primary radio operator, continues on to check in at the command bunker. Like desert reptiles, we try to locate a sliver of shade to crawl into; there is none, there is no escape. The grunts have spread ponchos over their foxholes in futile efforts to create shade; the dark green plastic absorbs the heat, turning the holes into steaming ovens. Most have abandoned their makeshift oases and seem to move about aimlessly through the sun's torment; like ragged zombies they wander without direction, always searching for the slightest hint of shade. The sun is torturing everyone and everything; it assaults not just our bodies but our minds as well. Inside the wire, the Marines live like prairie dogs. They sit in the entrances to the hot bunkers waiting for the next enemy round; when it arrives, everyone disappears underground.

The team leader returns; his face seems to have grown older in the brief time that he has been away from the team. He gives us the bad news, most of which we have heard from our hosts here at the mortar pit. There are large units of enemy troops between Con Thien and our objective; it is very doubtful that we will reach our assigned recon zone ... a firefight is very probable. Behind me someone asks why they want to send our team to find the enemy when they already have been plotted. The team leader (TL) just shakes his head while staring at the map; each team member wants to look at the map as if hoping to find a secret passage through the waiting enemy. We all agree to wait until just before dusk to leave; perhaps by doing so, we will not be spotted; none of us likes to move in the dark but we have little choice.

Before dusk we gather near the wire perimeter and reluctantly begin to move west toward the Devil and his whores. Already weak from the constant heat that has sucked the energy from us through the long day, we follow a reinforced squad of Marines west toward the blazing colors of the setting sun. The sky is filled with red-orange and blue-green, as bright yellow streaks bend from the mountain peaks in a dazzling spectacle. The Asian sun is not capable of compassion; the beauty that now fills the sky is merely a promise that it will return soon and bring with it the heat that tests our endurance and courage. The shirtless grunts are heavily armed, extra bandoliers of rifle ammo and machine gun belts are draped across their shoulders. We will move with them to a predetermined position where they will set up an ambush and listening post for the long night. The squad leader, a Corporal that looks Irish, is moving along with our team, he is looking at our map. We show him the route that we will follow and he continuously shakes his head while muttering obscenities directed toward the officers in the command bunker. He is the smallest and thinnest Marine in the squad, yet he is no doubt the alpha-male. It is obvious that none of the others would dare cross him for fear of his wrath. Like the others in the squad, months of red dust have been burned into his skin by the sun. On his ragged helmet cover that is decorated with the grenade pins of past battles, he has written "Chicago." Nothing else, just the one word. He tells us that he will keep the squad dug in until daylight. After that he will not allow them to be exposed to the North Vietnamese mortars. Our TL asks if the command bunker will keep him informed of our situation; the Corporal spews curses in the direction of the outpost and tells us that he never pays attention to them. He will have his radio operator monitor our frequency; he is obviously used to ignoring orders and making

18

decisions based on the welfare of his squad. Knowing that he can be trusted, we like him immediately. When we reach the ambush site, our team continues on, and as we pass through the ragged grunts each of them wishes us well; we try to hide our fear beneath the thick layers of black and green camo paint we have smeared across our faces. As we move on toward the waiting Devil, I glance back and see flashes as bright colors from the disappearing sun reflect from the shiny blades of worn entrenching tools and belts of machine gun ammo. The squad prepares their well-planned ambush with care. For those that enter the web of the killing zone, there will be no escape. The squad leader on one knee is watching us move away into the bush; he is smoking a last cigarette before the dark comes. Occasionally we can hear him give an order that is immediately carried out. From my position at the head of the column, I wave to him and he waves back.

As always, the interval between each man in the column is based on the terrain. In this ambush-prone scrub, we spread the interval until each man keeps the man ahead just in sight. Following some thirty meters behind me is the grenadier with the M-79 grenade launcher. Behind him is the TL who is followed closely by the primary radio operator. He is followed by the Corpsman who is followed by the secondary radio operator, the ATL (assistant team leader) is next and last and most important in this terrain is the rear point. We have all brought an extra complement of ammo for this patrol. In addition to the usual twenty magazines of twenty rounds each that I carry for my M-14, I also have two additional bandoliers stuffed into the cargo pockets of my trousers. Every man in our team is sure that we will find the enemy long before we reach the recon zone that we have been assigned to patrol for the next six days.

As we move west through the quiet, tomblike dusk, sounds become amplified; the heavy smell of death is around us and is growing stronger as we move. Soon I discover that the source of the overpowering stench is a shallow bomb crater positioned along our path; the crater was probably gouged into the earth by a five hundred pound bomb. There is a naked leg sticking out of the dark hole; on the foot is a rubber sandal made from a discarded truck tire. It looks as though the crater is moving … the movement is rats. In the dusk it looks like a blackish gray carpet covering the mangled, bloated bodies that the grunts have thrown into the hole. The bottom of the hole is full of large maggots that create the illusion that the crater is shimmering. I determine that there are at least twelve enemy bodies that lay intertwined in the crater. The huge rats are snapping at each other as they feed on the dead soldiers; this has to be the entrance to hell itself. The smell is overwhelming; it is so strong that I can taste it. There is a hideous face in the hole. It seems to be smiling at me. I move closer to investigate and I am not prepared to meet the horror that has beckoned to me. The smiling enemy soldier has no face, just a naked skull with the black hair and ears still intact; he is sitting upright, arms at his sides. I have never seen anything so repulsive, so horrid. A large black rat moves to the top of the head and at times his naked tail enters the empty eye sockets; the smile remains frozen in death. The rat, with flashing teeth, is snapping down at the others that try to join him on the bed of thick, black hair. I want to throw a grenade into the hole and destroy the horrible vision. I feel pity for the grinning enemy soldier; the rats have eaten his face. I will see his face for the rest of my life; he will visit me in the sweat-soaked dreams of a thousand nights. He will never leave me. He will become my companion … my demon.

As I back away from the edge of the crater, the grenadier who has quietly joined me grabs my shirtsleeve. He twists me around until I am facing him and he is staring into my eyes. Under the camo paint, his pale, trembling, face is a reflection of the revulsion we have just witnessed; do I also look like this? He pleads with me, "If I get wasted out there, for God's sake please don't leave me." I picture the grenadier with no face; my brain is in a panic from what I have seen. I assure him that we will all come back, and I pry his clamped fists from my jacket sleeve. The TL, annoyed that I have stopped moving, comes up and tells us harshly to move out. As he sees the horror in the crater he turns from the stinking mass and is suddenly overcome by nausea; I am already moving away as he empties his guts. I move fast to flee the smiling soldier; I will try to escape his stare for the rest of my life.

We continue west toward the Devil and his whores. After seeing the contents of the crater, I feel certain that we are now in the iron clutches of Satan. I try to put the horror out of my mind and concentrate on my job but it is no use; I need time to reason about the terrible scene but I can only push it into the deep recesses of my mind. Using the hedgerows as concealment, we are making very good time. The TL has told me to keep moving until I want to stop; it will be up to me. I want to get across the plantations quickly because it will be difficult to move undetected across this scrubland in the daylight. Finally I decide to stop, it is very dark and I can no longer see to move. We have traveled at least twelve hundred meters from the grunt ambush position. Soaked with sweat, we crawl into the thick brush of an old hedgerow to set in for the night. The rear point and I move out of the harbor site and place the Claymore mines where we think they will cause the most damage; when we return we hear whispers as the team leader and radio operators plot artillery on-call concentrations around our tiny perimeter. We lay in a circle, our weapons facing outward, our feet touching in the center; we resemble a wagon wheel. In the center are the two radios; each monitors a different frequency. The primary radio is set to communicate with the relay at Con Thien, who will send the hourly situation reports (sit-reps) to the Command in Dong Ha; the secondary radio is in contact with our artillery support. We box ourselves in with the artillery concentrations and pray that we do not need them. Two men will be awake at all times throughout the rest of the long night; I have drawn the third one-hour watch with the grenadier who is next to me. My pack is in front of me and my ammo belt is by my side; if we have to run I will leave the pack. My automatic rifle lies across the pack thrust through the thick brush pointing into the black of night. Exhausted and drained from the sun, I wrap myself into my poncho and fall asleep.

I think that I am dreaming because something is bumping my leg. When I wake, I realize that the primary radio operator is waking us up with his rifle butt; as I hear voices nearby in the dark, the team wakes up, one by one. It is black and I am disoriented; I have only my rifle to point the direction out from the harbor site in the direction of the hostile voices that are approaching. I can hear the

TL whispering into the radio handset to fire one of our on-call concentrations. In front of me I can only see a black void. I rub my eyes, I can't tell if they actually see, I rub and stare ... rub and stare.... If only I could see some light I would know that my eyes are actually working. Out to the front of my position I see a shadow, perhaps a silhouette. I can't tell if it is just another shade of the dark; I feel helpless. The shadow is moving, hunched over as if searching for the harbor site. Are my eyes working? I see it again, I am sure that it is an enemy soldier trying to probe toward us. I don't move and I try not to breathe; I worry that he can hear my heart as it pounds loudly in my ears. If I fire my rifle I will give away our position, yet if he keeps coming I will have to do something. I slip a grenade off of one of the four magazine pouches on my belt but then quickly realize that he is too close for the frag; I don't know what to do. My eyes hurt from the strain; I feel alone. The grenadier moves close and whispers that enemy soldiers are probing the other side of our perimeter, I whisper back that they are also in front of me. He tells me that the artillery is on the way. Now I see two shadows, they are bobbing up and down; my eyes hurt from the exertion, my teeth are clenched tight to prevent their chattering. Beneath my body I hear the rustling of dry leaves, perhaps it is a prowling centipede; a closer inspection reveals the noise is from my uncontrolled trembling. I am now reinforced by my ruthless companion— fear; he will allow no indecision, only reaction. I decide that if the shadows maintain their approach I will have to waste them with the rifle before they are able to toss a grenade into the midst of us; I will have no choice but to kill them both and give away our position. The phantoms continue moving toward me. My mind is racing now, I wonder if there is a round in the chamber of my weapon. I know that the weapon is locked and loaded but indecision is toying with me. I want to check the chamber in order to ensure my confidence; gently, without a sound, I ease the bolt back just enough to feel the smooth brass round with my thumb. I strain my ears for the sound of a grenade fuse. The selector is set to full automatic; my finger is on the safety. I think that a third shadow has appeared; I am not sure. I push against the safety with my trigger finger and aim at the approaching shadows; I will wait until the very last second before squeezing the trigger, they must not have time to return fire. I have never seen the world this dark.

There is a rumble in the distance, the TL whispers loudly ... "Shot" ... the first artillery round is on the way; seconds later he whispers ... "Splash" ... the round is five to ten seconds from impact. Everyone digs himself into the earth; we pray that the round is on target. I squirm to hide behind my pack and force myself into the dirt; the round is coming in like a freight train. Someone whispers frantically, "Oh God, it's close." The explosion rocks us; the confused enemy soldiers are screaming as another blows a whistle. They are desperate to find and close with us or the artillery will shred them. We know, and understand this tactic well. No one fires his weapon; the panicked enemy cannot locate us. An AK is popping wildly out in front of me; it is firing in all directions, they want us to return fire, they need to see a muzzle flash. I press myself deeper into the earth. The TL has ordered all on-call concentrations fired, he tells the battery to box us in. The screaming rounds come in fast from different directions; for the enemy grunts, there is no escape, there is no quarter, the hunted have become the hunters. The black night is punctuated with brilliant flashes that bore through our blinded eyes and deep into our brains. The world changes from deep black void to brilliant star white, faster and faster until a strobe effect is created that turns the deadly night into mindless confusion. Grotesque shadows, created from the flashes, dance through the harbor site changing shapes constantly. I can hear the calm voice of the radio operator clearly now. No longer whispering as he summons the artillery fire, carefully he walks the rounds toward our perimeter, adjusting the fire like an artist. As the rounds come closer, the overhanging tree limbs above us are cut by shell fragments and begin to fall. The stinking decayed earth that we try to embed ourselves into now blankets us as each blast sends a torrent of plantation dirt skyward and back down onto our position. More than one battery is firing now; I can hear the avenging rounds as they cross the sky from different directions. Like rag-dolls, we are tossed from the ground with each blast; I wait for the round that will find us. The noise is deafening and I place my hands over my ears, it does no good; pain shoots through my inner ear from the onslaught of each explosion. The artillery fire continues through the long night. Between blasts, I strain my eyes into the dark to see if the shadows are still there; I see nothing but the black void. The radio operator tells the TL that he is receiving a message from the relay. We are told to move back to the grunt ambush at dawn; they will be waiting for us and will provide support to cover our movement.

As dawn approaches, the TL asks for the artillery fire to be lifted and placed briefly on the route that we will take to the waiting Marines; the sudden silence enables me to hear the muted ringing in my ears. I am terrified to leave the harbor site; I am afraid to stay yet I am afraid to leave. We can't stay, the enemy will find us at daylight; they know where we are now because of where the artillery has been concentrated. The choice is a simple one. We have to move fast.

Before dawn we prepare to move. I dump the water from seven of the eight canteens that I carry; I want to be as light as possible. I also consider dumping the cans of rations but I don't want the enemy to get them. The TL gives the word for the Claymores to be blown. The two men that have been assigned that task hammer the levers on the "hellboxes" and wide screens of steel balls cut through the hedgerows grinding anything that offers resistance into mulch. I am given the word to move; as I exit the harbor site, I see that the ground is smoking from the hell that has been rained on it throughout the long night. There are no visible dead, but the area is littered with discarded equipment. Pieces of hot, smoking shell fragments are scattered across the area; we do not have time to search for bodies, our survival hinges on how rapidly we leave the area and cover the twelve hundred meters that separate us from the grunt ambush. As the sun rises, fleeting shadows are sent in vast numbers through the old plantation hedgerows; the shadows tease and taunt my senses that have been ravaged by the flash-filled darkness. Dawn is upon us; the Marine position cannot be too much farther ahead. The alarm comes from the rear point that we are being followed; then suddenly, from an M-16 comes the dreaded sound of a prolonged automatic burst. Instinctively, our column disintegrates to confuse the pursuing enemy; each man turns to fire a quick magazine. I concentrate on reaching the grunt position, nothing else matters. AK rounds are cracking through the air; I have quickened the pace to a fast trot. More fire is coming from behind; I hear more AK fire followed by M-16 bursts. Ahead of me, orange machine gun tracers are coming from the grunt ambush; the Marine that is firing the M-60 is peeking over a hedgerow dike. He stops firing and waves me over; as I wave back in acknowledgement, he quickly resumes firing. Seeing the other grunts firing from their fighting holes, I stop, turn, and kneel to help provide covering fire for the rest of the team. I fire into the dancing shadows, past my teammates that are staggered back at least fifty meters. I have fired well over a half dozen twenty-round magazines through the rifle on full auto; gray smoke pours from the hot weapon. The dripping sweat from my face sizzles on the hot steel and I can feel the heat of the barrel through my thick leather bush gloves; the familiar smell of burning rifle oil fills the air. I shift my covering fire to protect the grenadier as he lobs high explosive 40mm rounds into the undergrowth. The rear point passes us in a dead run yelling for us to come on, and I can hear the metallic rattle of empty rifle magazines in the cargo pockets of his trousers. The grunts continue firing as friendly mortars rip into the shadow filled brush. Exhausted, we move into the safety of the grunt ambush where I gulp down my canteen of water. The return fire fades and the order is passed from the Corporal to cease-fire. The adrenaline is pumping. We have no dead or wounded; we have once again tempted fate and have emerged unscathed. The squad leader sends a four-man fire team in the direction of Con Thien as the point element. He knows what he is doing; when ordered, the remaining fire teams and machine gun crew withdraw in perfect order. The squad leader joins us; we tell him about the long night of close artillery fire. He seems amused and once again hurls curses at the troops in the rear. As we move, he maintains constant order within the column; he is a good Marine. Moving back to the wire at Con Thien, we thank the grunts for helping us. We are returning to Dong Ha soon so we give them all of our cigarettes, long-range rations, candy, and canned fruit; it is all we have that is of any value.

Later that evening as we clean our weapons, someone produces a bottle of whiskey; we pass it around, each man taking a deep drink. I drink to forget the picture in my mind of the rat-chewed corpse in the crater; the image will forever be my constant companion. The whiskey does no good; I will never forget—the faceless enemy soldier won't let me. I have learned that there are things worse than just dying. The next patrol order will be issued for us soon. There is no time to reason.

4

Hunger

The summer heat at Con Thien has become horrendous. I am unable to quench the constant thirst with the warm, plastic flavored canteen water. As a canteen-full is drained and absorbed, the water quickly pours from us. The sweat soaks through our clothes and into our packs and ammo pouches. Across the napalm-scarred plantations, the searing sun is relentless; there is no shade, no escape. We carry additional canteens but there is a price; the extra weight seems to demand additional water consumption. I decide to carry eight canteens, while some other team members carry nine and yet others carry only six. We refill the canteens when water is located; most often it is foul, polluted and stagnant. Purification tablets are added to the thick, fetid soup to kill amoebas and the other parasites that will bore holes through the lining of our stomachs. The tablets add a distinct iodine flavor that blends with the plastic and the odor of bacteria; the result is a taste so horrible that drinking becomes a task. At times it is difficult to keep it down.

Our seven-man team is being sent back into the DMZ from Con Thien. We are to rendezvous with a platoon from Alpha Company, 1st Battalion 9th Marine Regiment and follow them as they sweep northwest toward the Ben Hai River. At a predetermined point within the boundaries of our recon zone, the platoon will turn back to the southeast and move back toward Con Thien, leaving us well hidden. After they have moved away from us, we will move deep into our RZ, which covers six grid-squares and stretches north from the "4- nineties" along the Ben Hai.

The night before we leave for Con Thien, we are introduced to a civilian freelance newspaper photographer who has asked to come along. This is very unusual; he must have approached some very high-ranking officials for permission. We are reluctant to take him along; he has no training and will be unarmed. He has been on operations with both Army and Marine units farther to the south but this is an entirely different facet of the war; recon patrols into the DMZ are very hazardous. As we arrange and re-arrange the food and equipment in our heavy packs, he sits among us taking photos. He tells us about the war to the south and how the fighting along the DMZ, fought exclusively by Marines, is the most coveted arena for a reporter to cover. It is very difficult for them to reach this remote area and of those that have come, many have been wounded or killed. He has spent time with the Air Cavalry to the south, which for a reporter is the most easily accessed unit in Vietnam. As he rambles on with stories of operations that we have never heard of, we grin knowingly at one another and pretend to be interested. We know that this is not the war that is being fought to the south; this is much different. Our under-strength division is fighting on two borders and we are at the very end of the long supply line. This is not the war that reaches the living rooms of America each evening. Silently, we are not sure if we should respect his courage or question his sanity.

We arrive at Con Thien; the blowtorch heat is like a humid oven. Sweat pours from our bodies that are bent forward straining against the straps of our heavy packs. We immediately move away from the perimeter of the tiny outpost toward the platoon of grunts that we will follow. Above us, the sky is ablaze with the blinding rays from a pitiless sun. There is no beauty here, only destruction. At times the heat is visible; it rises from the baked earth in transparent waves. As I breathe, the stench of unburied dead and human waste mixes with the heated air that fills my lungs. Moving toward the waiting platoon, we pass through an old bivouac area that is littered with discarded C-Ration cans and rotting sandbags. I kick through the trash looking for anything of value that may have been

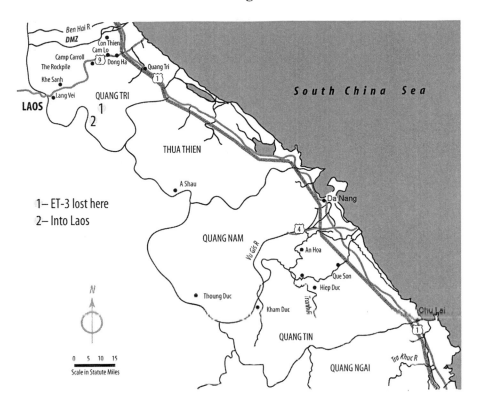

I Corps Tactical Zone. This northern area of South Vietnam was origi-
nally held by the Third Marine Division in Quang Tri and Thua Thien
Provinces. The First Marine Division held Quang Nam, Quang Tin and
Quang Ngai Provinces; Special Forces camps were scattered throughout the area as well. In early 1968, as the war escalated the Marines while
moving the bulk of their 3rd Division troops farther north were reinforced by a host of tough U.S. Army units. Most notably were the elite
101st Airborne, the newly formed Americal Division and a vast number
of support troops. Two particular units that distinguished themselves in
I Corps were the 3rd Battalion 21st Infantry "Gimlets" and the 196th
Light Infantry Brigade.

accidentally left behind; all Marines and soldiers do this, perhaps
scavenging is part of the warrior creed. Near an old half-filled fighting hole I have found a beautiful flower. Like a rare jewel, it seems
misplaced; there is no place for beauty here. The team continues
on as I pause to admire the bright colors that seem so refreshing,

29

so radiant. It is the first beautiful thing that I have seen in the ravaged plantations. I remove the sweat soaked leather bush glove from my hand and drop to one knee to touch the delicate petals. My hand is caked with slippery mud, a mixture of red dust from Route 9 and sweat; the hand seems filthy and crude against the soft purple and white flower. I decide not to touch it; I do not want to spoil this last bit of beauty and purity that has somehow escaped the Devil's grasp. The sun-scorched, war-ravaged plantations refuse to die; defiantly, they have struggled to place this tiny bit of color as an offering of peace or perhaps to represent hope. I look toward the team that continues to move on without me; I am reluctant to leave the petite blossom unprotected. Quickly, I gather a small pile of rusty ration cans and place them around the frail green stem. Perhaps the cans will offer protection; the team is looking back at me, I have to rejoin them. I want to take the flower with me but it will only wither and die in the heat. I have done all that I can to protect it from the madness. For a brief moment, I have escaped the hell of war and entered a peaceful sanctuary where care and compassion still exist. Now I must resume my charge in this napalm-burned asylum; the kind hand that offered care to the helpless once again becomes the hand of a killer. As I move away from the little pile of rusty cans, occasionally I look back; with each glance the soft colors of the flower fade until they blend into the dry-green of the tortured vegetation.

I am assigned as rear point but because of the intense heat, I will alternate with my friend at the point position. The heat and thick humid underbrush will strip the life from us just as it has stripped the life from the ravaged, shell-scarred earth. As we move, the reporter seems bewildered, or perhaps lost in thought; I wonder why he has entered into this hell, this nightmare, he is obviously intelligent, why is he here? I remind myself that it is none of my business; only he knows those answers. If we are to die together in the DMZ, it is our destiny and nothing more. Silently, I wonder if both life and death are prearranged; if so, are we to die with certain people? Does fate route the paths of our lives until meeting as strangers we face death and destiny together? I stop myself from thinking; the heat has caused my mind to drift. Here along death's threshold, questions and emotions must be placed aside and forced into boxes with tight lids; the boxes must not be reopened here. If we survive, the boxes may be opened and the contents examined someday ... but not here.

When we reach the grunt position we find that they are waiting impatiently for us and without a pause, we immediately begin to move across the overgrown hedgerows of the plantations. We move in three columns; there are flanker columns along each side of the center column to prevent ambush. The worn out grunts are exhausted after months of patrolling this jungle wasteland. The sun has transformed their skin into burned leather; under their helmets are the faces of renegade aborigines. Shirtless, they travel light and anything that is not used daily has been discarded; I envy the light loads that they carry. It is obvious they have very little use for us and they seem annoyed that we are with them.

We move all day and when the sun begins to fade, a perimeter is established. Our team will sleep near a shallow bomb crater; we hope that it will offer protection from the enemy mortars that may arrive during the night. The warm night is uneventful. We sit in the bomb crater sharing whispered conversation with the reporter. The black, cloudless sky is filled with brilliant stars that sparkle like white diamonds; occasionally long, bright streaks of white fire plunge to earth from the jewel-crusted heavens. As we watch the beauty of the meteor shower, whispers become sporadic and questions drift through the crater unanswered as each of us falls into deep sleep. When we wake; the feint glow of the rising sun promises to turn the world ablaze as brilliant colors streak across the dark gray-blue morning sky. The platoon is already moving. We dread the deadly heat that will soon be upon us; when it arrives, there will be no mercy, no quarter, and no escape. The column continues northwest without stopping and passes through a heavily bombed area filled with enemy trench-lines and bunkers. When we stop for a rest, one of our team finds a Chinese gas mask. It is the first that any of us has ever seen and I wonder why it is here. The primitive mask is made of a poor quality green rubber. A hose that resembles an elephant's trunk hangs from the front; a canister is attached to its end, someone cuts it up with a Ka-Bar knife. After a mere five minutes of rest, the platoon is once again on the move. We help each other back into the heavy packs and take our place in the column; none of us has ever felt heat so intense. By noon we have reached the light red line that meanders across our map marking the DMZ. Turning south, the platoon will continue on toward Con Thien as we stray from the procession, moving deep into the heavy underbrush. As we are left behind on the lonely, hostile border, no one speaks and no one waves to us. Like ghosts of the aborigine warriors that they resemble, the grunts silently fade back into the bush; as visible waves of heat rise from the ground, the scene becomes surreal, as if they are being absorbed back into the wretched wilderness.

Our team quickly turns due west, moving deeper into our recon zone toward the Ben Hai River. The slowly flowing tributary that forms the border with North Vietnam also crosses the western edge of our RZ. Every member of the team knows that at this very instant, we are probably the northernmost American unit in South Vietnam; there is nothing to the north or west but the enemy homeland. The devastating heat is at times punishing. It pounds and beats us while burning through the wide, floppy brims of our bush hats. The blistering steel barrels of our rifles cannot be touched with a naked hand and the water in our plastic canteens is very warm. We will move through this inferno for at least five days, searching for any infiltrating enemy units that threaten the outpost at Con Thien with ground assault. The regiments of North Vietnamese that are poised just across the border can quickly cross the shallow elephant fords of the Ben Hai undetected and maneuver their assault battalions into position. It was across these same shallow, hidden, manmade fords that mighty elephant armies moved south to attack the Cham and it was across these same crossings that the Le forces attacked the Nguyen Wall. And now, the ancient fords are crossed by their descendents; the same determined masses that once fought to dominate the southern regions hundreds of years before have once again returned to lay claim to the prize.

After moving for two hours through the heat, I am signaled forward; the point must be exhausted. Moving along the spread out column, I pass my sweat soaked teammates and pat each on the shoulder; bent forward to rest their packs high on their backs, they can only nod in reply. There is no canopy and the sun beats into the steamy high underbrush and elephant grass with a vengeance. As I pass the reporter, it is obvious that he knows he has made a terrible mistake. He is bent forward, a canteen in his hand and forcing a smile; I tell him that it will only get worse and he nods in agreement. Sweat pours from the brim of my saturated bush hat in a steady stream. Knowing that I must replace the sweat with water if I am going to last through the day, I drink from the hot canteen while moving toward the head of the column. The point is sitting with his rifle across his lap gasping for breath; the sweat has stopped and he is obviously approaching heat exhaustion. Leaves and grass stains are caked on his wet clothes; spiders crawl across his bush hat and his face is streaked with blood from the punctures of thorns. Brushing the spiders from him, I pour my canteen over his head and down his back under the heavy pack; like the others, he can only nod as a gesture of thanks. The team leader points the direction and reluctantly, I move ahead into the wall of thick brush. I can only weave my way through the elephant grass and thorns; a machete would make too much noise. As I push ahead, the tall grass quickly closes behind me like a trap; I cannot see the man that follows. Worried that I may be shot by my own men; I signal the team leader forward. Our team leader is a Canadian and one of the best Marines any of us will ever know. Suddenly, he appears through the wall of high grass and vines; the wall closes behind him and we are isolated together in a steamy pocket. Having stopped, I am on fire as the salty sweat enters the hundreds of cuts made by the sharp elephant grass and thorns. The sweat also burns my eyes, making it difficult to see. I remove the leather bush gloves and try to wipe my eyes but the effort only makes them burn with more intensity; now both tears and sweat stream down my face. The team leader wants to close the interval between each of us; we have to get through this thick bush before we begin to obtain heat casualties. He tells me to move as fast as possible but to be careful, after a quick glance at my compass, I push on through the ever-present wall. At times I use my rifle to push down the mass of green; I hold the M-14 in my outstretched arms and fall forward. The grenadier then

July 1967. Near the Ben Hai River our tired team takes a break from the heat and vines. Left to right: Fred Anderson, Joe Fink, and the author. Never out of reach is the author's automatic M-14 "Little Queenie" (courtesy of Arthur Loder).

steps into the little opening and helps me stand up; again, I repeat the process inching ahead into the entanglement. After moving for two hours, it is doubtful we have traversed a full one hundred meters. Dark approaches and we move the team into a small perimeter; each man mashes down as much of the brush as possible until the eight of us occupy a circle that is less than ten feet in diameter. I am too tired to help place the Claymores; collapsed in a sweat soaked heap, I force the heavy humid air deep into my lungs and gulp down the warm plastic flavored water. I can hear the shutter coming from the camera of the reporter; he is getting his money's worth. Radio watches are assigned and artillery on-calls plotted. I am too tired to eat and I decide not to bother with my poncho; I will sleep in the matted brush. Using the hard pack for a pillow, I clutch the M-14 across my chest. The TL passes a half smoked cigarette to me and I take a number of deep drags; it tastes good. The bush has taken my strength. I promise myself that I will eat something before we move. The merciful dusk extinguishes the fire of the sun and we are thankful; the quiet dark is soon upon us. I pull the salt-crusted bush hat over my face. Soon sleep will transport me to the peaceful haven where the fragile flower soothed me with hope and beauty.

The night passes fast and as the first rays of the demon sun appear, we wolf down cold rations and prepare to continue north. Once again the point leads the column; as he passes me out of the matted clearing, he merely shakes his head. I quietly remind him not to push it too hard; nodding in agreement, he disappears into the wall of grass and vines. As each man leaves the clearing, the brush springs back toward the morning sky until I find myself alone and isolated, just as it was when I first stopped here a few hours before. With the green ration cans buried, there is no visible evidence that we have harbored here. We continue on through the dew-drenched morning and as the sun grows hot it burns into the wet grass, turning the cool wet dew into steam that forcefully displaces the balmy night air. By mid-morning we are again trapped in the humid inferno and well before noon, I am again signaled forward to relieve the exhausted point. He has not waited for me and I meet him halfway along the column; his clothes are torn and he is again caked in green from insects, thorns and leaf fragments. As we pass, he whispers that it is rougher than the day before; I hesitate to move ahead where the wall of bush is waiting and I pray that there will soon be a break.

By mid-afternoon I have emerged from the sea of tangled brush. I am able to move more freely now and the heat is not quite so ruthless. The interval between each team member is adjusted and as we move I can only see the grenadier that follows twenty feet behind. Before dusk, the point comes forward to help me search for a harbor site and together we move toward a thicket that is surrounded by fallen trees. Satisfied that it is a defendable position, we signal the team ahead. The team sets in for the night and rations are opened. I am worried about my water; I have used more canteens than usual moving through the thick brush. I am not alone; we will search for water when the sun returns. As the dusk engulfs our harbor site, wild thrashing comes from the TL. He is crawling from the thicket dragging his equipment. Soon the entire team is scrambling from under the overhanging branches that are crawling with bamboo vipers. The small, arrow-headed, green snakes seem to be everywhere. The Claymores are gathered and we move away from the venomous vipers, sliding into a dry bomb crater that is surrounded by elephant grass. After the Claymores are placed, I open my pack and search through the contents with my Ka-Bar. I want to make sure that it is safe to be digging around in the dark pack for a can of rations; the pack would make a good home for a snake. All through the long night we think of the nearby-infested tree while North Vietnamese and American artillery duel across the DMZ; the rounds from both opponents often passing directly above us. The night is filled with brilliant flashes and rumbling that makes sleep difficult. As the morning approaches, everyone is already awake and prepared to search for a source of water.

We have moved only a short distance when the point finds a bomb crater; it contains algae covered rainwater that is old and stagnant. I crawl into the stinking crater with him and the canteens are passed to us. As the team provides security, we devise a method to get through the slime and algae to the water. Using my hands and forearms, I spread the green mat apart and the point quickly dips the canteen beneath the cleared surface. I allow the mat of algae to close over the submerged canteen and after the bubbles have stopped, the mat is once again spread and the point removes the canteen. Repeating this method, we fill at least three canteens for each of the eight men. Finished, I scrub my slime-covered hands with the red bomb crater dirt. It does not remove the slime, instead the red dirt and green algae turns into larvae infested mud; it will soon be removed by sweat. We slide out of the crater and crawl back into the brush to join the waiting team. Tablets are added to the water and along with whispered curses I can hear the sounds of long gulps and spitting as the thirsty team drinks and spits out wiggling mosquito larvae. Without speaking, the team leader nods to the point and we continue the day's hunt into the inferno of the DMZ.

Our adversary is close; we are finding the evidence that betrays his concealment and announces his presence. The flat scrub-covered plantations have suddenly been transformed into vine-choked dry streambeds and deep ravines. To our west a short distance flows the Ben Hai; we are less than a kilometer from the homeland of our enemy. There is no escape from the humid vegetation that drains both body and mind. At times, I am certain that it is possible for our team to be consumed by the enveloping walls of foliage; without a trace we could easily disappear forever, absorbed into the tangled mass. This is our fourth day; hopefully, we have only two left. To the east we hear a single rifle shot. The team stops and moves into a tight perimeter—perhaps our presence has been discovered. The enemy will often signal to one another with a single shot but never a second. It is difficult to determine where a single shot has originated but a second shot will always reveal the position.

The team is well hidden in the thick brush. There is no true canopy above to create shade; the sun blazes into our perimeter, it becomes suffocating among the bomb-splintered trees and thorns. I have removed my pack and I use it to rest my rifle across. Staring into the green wall of bush, I am only able to see a mere five meters; the jungle is a "cat's cradle" of twisted vines that seem alive, as if reaching for me. Sometimes, even when not moving, I find myself held in their grasp, it as if they silently attack when I am not looking, as though they are thinking organisms. When moving, the only way to pass through the vines is to become a vine; it is impossible to push through the jungle, forcing, fighting, and struggling. The bush must be negotiated with and each vine must be silently dealt with as an individual. Stealth and quiet is all that prevents our destruction from the ever-present enemy. We have learned that we must become a part of the bush, always searching for the passage that lies hidden through the entanglement; at times, the sharp blade of a Ka-Bar must create the passage. Each step and each movement must be carefully planned, each twist of the heavy pack must be done as to prevent entrapment.

We have heard no additional rifle shots so we continue on to the north. I am again called forward to relieve the point and as we pass he whispers that North Vietnamese are everywhere. I nod in agreement and continue on toward the head of the column. We move north for the rest of the day and as dusk approaches, we turn to the east; I am low on water. Below is a stream that has been blasted into a series of craters that have turned the once clear water into the familiar stagnant slime that we have become accustomed to consuming. I ask the TL if he wants to move down to it and fill canteens. He seems lost in thought, he does not answer. He is staring at the stream as if he has seen something. I drop to one knee and aim the rifle toward the direction he is looking. He must have seen something, he points into the thick jungle above and behind; I immediately turn and move away from the ambush that may be waiting below. We find a thick stand of bamboo. Weaving our way into the heart of the fragrant green stalks, we form a tight perimeter that will be our harbor site for the night. The team has very little water but just below is an endless supply that teases us. It calls to us, like a siren—as our lips dry and our tongues thicken, we will be tempted. Below us, the rancid oasis is a killing zone; our enemy has laid claim to the only water in this area of our RZ. We will have to search for another source. The TL has spotted the enemy grunts below, we will move away when the sun returns. The night is long and I force myself not to drink; the small amount of crawling bomb crater water in my canteen is now more precious than its weight in diamonds. A few meters below our position, the enemy has moved all night, perhaps stopping to fill canteens before continuing on to the east. We have not called for artillery; to do that would advise the enemy that a recon team has infiltrated into their domain. When the sun returns and we are once again consumed by the heat and jungle, we will suffer. Without the foul crater water, the team will soon be burdened with heat casualties.

It is our fifth day and we are moving to the east toward the glow of the new day. The jungle is still sleeping as we move. We must find water ... it is critical. The sun sends the heat, it grows and becomes what we have dreaded and expected yet have not quite prepared for. The heat builds as it sucks the life from everything it encounters. I pray that we will be extracted the following day. At mid-morning I relieve the point; as we pass along the column, he asks if I have any water left. He has used his while moving against the wall of vines. The heat has sapped his strength; I share the last of my water with him. As I move ahead I hold the canteen upside down, the rest of the team is shaking their heads; there is no water in any of their canteens. The TL tells me to move south, perhaps there will be a crater along the way. The sun burns into us and our mouths are dry. I have slowed my pace; each vine becomes a task. The sweat has stopped and I am becoming dizzy; I am certain that soon I will collapse. Behind me the team is fighting the thirst while searching into the jungle for signs of the enemy. Below us in a dark ravine drifts the rotten-egg smell of stagnant water. The TL comes forward and decides to send the point down to investigate; I am too dizzy to go with him, instead I set up my rifle to provide covering fire as he moves alone down into the bomb blasted abyss. He covers the few meters quickly and after scouting the ravine, signals us down. The water smells terrible; it has the stench of death, the same odor that is present as gas escapes from a bloated body. I help the others fill the canteens. Every canteen must be filled, we have no idea when we will find water again. Like a harbor site, a water source is never visited a second time. Adding tablets to the canteens, I drink as much of the foul-infested slime as possible. I refill each quart canteen as it is emptied until my stomach is stretched. I am sure that I have swallowed countless larvae; I no longer care. As we begin to move from the ravine, I feel the water being absorbed into my body and restoring my strength. The secondary radio operator grabs my sleeve and turns me toward something across the cratered stream that is partially hidden in the shadows. I have to look twice to believe what I am seeing; it is the arm of a dead enemy soldier. He is half submerged in the water from which we have filled the canteens. Nausea comes over me but my stomach is empty, there is nothing to come up; the water has already entered into my body. We look at each other and can only shake our heads and whisper frustrated curses. The rest of the team has spotted the corpse. We are sure that the enemy has done this intentionally; perhaps they think we will not drink water that is polluted by their dead. There are no options. Without water we will die. Slowly, I raise the plastic canteen, I close my eyes and holding my breath I allow the foul liquid to surge into me; tears of frustration now flow into the streams of sweat. I place the experience into a box and seal it. We move away from the ravine, continuing south.

As dusk approaches we move into a defendable harbor site. We are not sure when our extraction will take place. Tomorrow will be our sixth day. Each team member does a quick inventory of their rations; there is very little left, perhaps one meal per man. The TL notifies the relay of our situation, water is scarce, food is critical and we have located enemy troops in all areas of the RZ. With the dark comes the welcomed break in the heat; our bodies will gather strength and prepare for the searing assault from the sun. As canteens are opened, the smell of death engulfs us. No one thinks about it, we drink the water that was so difficult to locate. The sounds of long bubbling drinks from the canteens fill the harbor site; the sounds of spitting have long stopped, the bits of leaves and mosquito larva are now consumed with the stagnant fluid. All through the night North Vietnamese move past us ... no one sleeps. We send reports to the relay advising them of the enemy movement. Dawn approaches and we begin our move toward Con Thien. There will be no extraction by helicopter.

As the heat returns we maintain our movement to the east. In the distance, perhaps two kilometers to the east, the sound of a massive firefight is ripping through the heat-drenched morning. The TL moves us into a perimeter and both radios are busy sending and receiving, hunting for any available information. We will have to move south to avoid the escalating fight. No details are sent to us, we are told to remain in our RZ and stay until ordered to leave. The TL reminds them that we have no food left and that there is very little water in our area. They know our situation and the order is repeated: "Stay until relieved." We are not sure which way to move, the enemy is everywhere. To the east the fight has become a continuous rattle of rifle and machine gun fire, punctuated with blasts from artillery and mortars. The grunts have found a sizable force and we wonder if the enemy soldiers that have moved past us each night have joined in the battle. The firing continues, at times there is a lull but it quickly builds again; jets have arrived and cross our position with their afterburners ablaze. The ear-shattering blasts from their expended ordnance fills the air. The ground quakes as bombs find enemy targets. There is no end to it and now the fighting has come closer, so close that at times rounds from Chinese and Russian 12.7mm heavy machine guns pass near us. We have to move; a recon team cannot remain in one place for very long. The point leads us from the perimeter, we are moving west, away from Con Thien, away from food and clean water.

We move through the heat well into dusk before finding a harbor site. We have had no food since early morning. It will be a long, hungry night. The water in our canteens tastes even more horrible without food to go with it; perhaps it is fermenting as the stagnant water that smells of death is heated in the plastic canteens. Most of the team has brought enough cigarettes to last for two weeks; those that do not smoke will grow even hungrier without the appetite-suppressing nicotine. The reporter looks lost, yet we have come to respect and even admire his endurance. He is much older than we, yet he is able to keep up and seldom complains about the heat. To pass the time before dark, he tells us about his girlfriend who is waiting for him in Saigon. They came to Vietnam together to cover the war as freelance reporters and photographers. We were to be back at Dong Ha by now; he will not arrive at their hotel in Saigon on schedule, he tells us she will be worried. I assure him that we will be extracted very soon; they will not leave us in the bush with no food. He tries with great determination to drink the canteen water but he has not grown used to the stagnant flavor and odor as we have. I feel pity for him; he is a good person and should not be here in this very worst part of the war, hungry and drinking water that has been intentionally polluted with rotten corpses. I have a last cigarette before the dark turns the world into a black void. Tonight there will be no food to supply the energy needed to carry the packs when the sun returns. I wonder where we will find the strength.

During the night the enemy is again near us, moving east toward the fighting. North Vietnamese artillery is firing at Con Thien from a position nearby and the TL calls for a fire mission. The rounds scream in and suddenly the jungle is filled with the bright flashes of secondary explosions. We have hit the target; its magazine is exploding. The enemy has stopped firing at Con Thien. Now they will search for us. They know that we are here—we have slapped them across the face to announce our presence. They now know that a recon team is prowling the area; the fire mission has ended a phase of our patrol and opened a fresh one. The team can no longer hope to remain hidden. We must now bring artillery and jets into the duel. We are no longer able to depend on stealth alone to counter the enemy threat. We will use aggression and speed in order to survive.

Throughout the night we stare into the black void; each sound is amplified. As the first hint of the new day filters through the thick bush, we begin to move. It is our seventh day. As we move I feel the first true hunger pang and as the day progresses, I find that only the nicotine from the cigarettes is helping manage the weight of the heavy pack. By noon I am called forward to relieve the exhausted point. As we pass, I ask if he has any rations left, he has nothing. He asks how many packs of cigarettes I have; I remind him that I have almost a full carton. There will be cigarettes if there is nothing else. As I take my place at the head of the column and move through the vines, my empty stomach feels raw. We continue back into the RZ and away from the fighting that has now moved to the southeast. The jets have not stopped making bomb runs since the battle began the day before. Twice during the day I halt the team due to enemy movement; I have heard their voices and the sounds of rattling equipment as if they are in a hurry to either join the fighting or perhaps to flee. Before dusk the point relieves me to search for a harbor site. I help place the Claymores and smoke one cigarette after the next to kill the hunger. The pangs are becoming intense. We have burned a great deal of energy that has not been replaced. I crave a chocolate bar covered with peanut butter; I have to stop thinking about food because it will only make things worse than they are. The night arrives and we are too hungry to sleep; each of us prays that an extraction will arrive before we become too weak to move with our gear. I decide that I will abandon my pack if I continue to be drained; I don't care what the consequences are, the Marine Corps can send me a bill for it.

The night passes slowly. The enemy once again feels our sting as we lash out with artillery. Again the North Vietnamese quit firing on Con Thien as we send volleys of eight inch and 155mm across the border, into their lair. They will search harder for us; our fire missions are preventing them from neutralizing the defenses of the tiny outpost. I am sure that we will be extracted when the sun rises.

Dawn welcomes our eighth day in the DMZ. I wake to massive hunger pangs that are very painful. The stagnant water and cigarettes do little to stop the pangs as they claw into the walls of my empty stomach. I have lost track of when I ate my last can of rations. It must have been at least two days before; I will ask one of the others—perhaps they remember. I have trouble lifting the heavy pack. Though it contains no cans of rations, it seems to have grown heavier. The point begins to move from the harbor site, we have turned back to the east, toward Con Thien. I hope that we will keep moving, all the way across the plantations; perhaps along the way we can scavenge for discarded rations or abandoned enemy chow. The thought of finding a basket of rice balls soaked in the pungent fermented fish sauce, *nuoc mam*, causes my mouth to water and my guts to growl.

We move through the hot day; the point and I relieve one another more often as the heat and hunger sap our strength like parasites. At times we are forced to hide from enemy troops that seem to be moving north. The jets continue to attack the enemy units and some of the air strikes are now to our west along the Ben Hai. We agree that the enemy is withdrawing and with the battle finished, we will be extracted soon. The team is suffering; we must have food to continue our evasion of the searching patrols. I worry that if we are forced into a running fight, we will not have the energy to escape. As dark approaches we lose all hope of an extraction. We are enjoying a last smoke when the radio operator announces that we will be extracted the following morning by helicopter. Throughout the night we watch and listen as enemy units move past. They seem to be burdened with equipment that we soon determine is possibly their wounded comrades; they are moving north with their wounded. All night long we call artillery into the fleeing enemy troops. I fantasize that they are carrying rice and vegetables, perhaps salted dried fish that makes my mouth water. I think of luscious pineapples and overripe mangoes that lay discarded along the path of the enemy retreat. Thoughts of food fill my mind to the point of obsession. I have never felt true hunger before; it is my first experience with the demon. I think of the coming extraction and finding rations aboard the chopper—I can hardly wait for the dawn. Mercifully, sleep comes over me.

I wake to find my teammates have gathered the Claymores and are preparing to search for an LZ. I am weak from the hunger; the cigarettes do little to stop the pangs. Everyone is eager to move. Speech comes in excited rapid-fire whispers that have no pattern. I pull the pack onto my shoulders and with the rifle cradled in my arms, I follow the others as thoughts of chocolate bars and strong, hot coffee take flight through my brain. As we move I notice that the point has changed directions. The word comes back to me that our extraction has been cancelled. I am distraught and overcome with frustration; I send silent curses to those that have kept us here. The TL moves us into a thicket, where we will stay while he sorts things out. Messages are sent advising our rear area that we have not had food in days. The stagnant water in our canteens is almost gone; there will be no more water. We know that the enemy now has the few water holes guarded; they will wait for thirst to drive us to them, and their ambush will destroy the recon team that has been such a problem to their efforts. There is little that we can do. It is our ninth day and the beginning of our fourth or fifth day without food ... no one is sure when we last ate. The team is too weak to continue moving, yet if we stop, the enemy will find us. We decide to remain here and fight; there will be ambushes scattered throughout the entire RZ, and we may be too light-headed to find them. We form a tight perimeter. Across the ravine just below us is an old agricultural area that will be our LZ when the time comes. We will stay here until we are extracted; no one has the strength to continue on. The heat and hunger have stripped us of our reserves. I locate some tender leaves on a small tree and try to get them down but I am unable to swallow. My body will not allow them to enter my stomach; I try again, it will not go down. I peel bark from the tree with my Ka-Bar and manage to get some of it down. It does not stay down very long; it comes up in a painfully twisted mass that leaves my throat raw. The team is searching for protein—there are no insects, no grubs. After months of cursing them there is not a bug to be found. Perhaps they have recognized our ravenous state and have fled. I ask the Corpsman how long we can last without food. His answer is not what I want to hear; we can last for an indefinite amount of time and those that are keeping us out here know that. His concern is that we are almost out of water, that is another thing entirely. In this heat, we must have water. We worry that if we are extracted we will not have the strength to reach the chopper. I promise myself that I will get to the helicopter; if I have to leave my equipment, I will get aboard. Someone has asked the Corpsman if his plasma is edible. He tells us that it is protein and we can have a container if we want it. We all look at one another and it is decided that together we will force it into our systems. Perhaps with the added fuel we will have a fresh supply of energy. He takes one of the many containers from his pack and opens it. Inside, the plasma is in a clear plastic bag with an I.V. tube attached. When he cuts the bag open the smell is overpowering. We expected something quite different. Instantly we have changed our minds; as the stench moves through the jungle, one of the team digs a hole with his Ka-Bar and buries the bag before the enemy troops notice it. We had no idea that plasma smelled so bad. The Corpsman tells us that we are not hungry yet; when we are truly hungry we will not hesitate to eat something just because it smells bad. Whenever Marines find themselves in these predicaments, it is the Navy Corpsmen that step forward to keep the others going. They never complain about how tough things are, they take it in stride and continue on.

We have stayed in this place for far too long, but there is nowhere else to move without meeting enemy patrols. As dusk approaches, we move across the ravine to the edge of the clearing that will be our LZ if the extraction ever comes. The night is filled with endless sounds of nearby troop movement. A column is moving along the ravine that we crossed. I wonder if they will find the buried plasma bag. We let the enemy pass; they are too close for artillery. Reports are sent to the relay giving the details of their movement. Jets will deal with them when the sun returns. I am too hungry to sleep so I sit up all through the night listening to the enemy soldiers stumble on the loose rocks in the ravine. When the first hint of dawn sends an eerie glow from the east, we move to a position along the LZ. It is our tenth day, our fifth day without food. As we move, I notice that the pangs have left. Perhaps the Corpsman is right, maybe we really are not hungry yet. We move into a thicket and wait for daylight. I search the trees for vipers; the little snakes would make a fine breakfast. I have reached the point of eating raw bamboo viper.

The radio operator tells us that the extraction choppers are on the way. We have sent the coded position of the LZ; now we just wait and pray that the enemy grunts have moved away from the ravine. To our south we hear the familiar popping sounds of the turbine engines and waves of excitement come over us. The hunger is suddenly forgotten—we have found a reserve of strength. The Claymores are collected and we move to the edge of the clearing; the sugary pineapples that once covered the LZ left long ago. In the distance, we see the escort gun ships as they approach abreast of one another; their rockets and machine guns will clear the tree lines that surround the LZ. Much higher in the clouds, Phantoms circle waiting to be summoned, their wings filled with "snake and nape," their cannons loaded with 20mm. Adrenaline is mixing with the hunger pangs that have suddenly returned with vengeance; I am becoming light-headed. I am no longer in control of myself; I am merely reacting.

Two CH-46 troopships are directly over us as the gun ships begin to make machine-gun runs along the tree lines that frame the clearing. Their orange tracers tear into the jungle that offers concealment to enemy gunners. We are told to move onto the clearing and throw a yellow smoke grenade to mark our position. The lead gun ship pilot sees more than one group of people below, so we must identify ourselves before they can send the troopship into the LZ. After the smoke is thrown, the gun ships fire rockets across our heads into the tree line; without waiting for the enemy grunts to be driven away, the lead troopship materializes from nowhere and turns the opened cargo ramp toward us with both gunners firing into suspected enemy positions. Surprised by the sudden appearance, we run toward the helicopter that barely touches the ground. There is nothing left, the strength is gone, we are moving in slow motion;

the distance seems so great ... I am so weak. The reporter is beside me and we grab onto each other, pulling and pushing the other through the rotor blast. The hot turbine exhaust fills our lungs as we struggle toward the opened ramp; we never let go. If one of us falls, we both fall, if one takes a round the other will drag him.

I look behind, the point is following us; he drags his heavy pack by a strap with one hand while aiming his M-16 at the tree line with the other, his face is turned and contorted as the rotors blast debris into his eyes and mouth. Firing has erupted from all sides of the clearing. I worry that the chopper will have to leave—it is taking hits. We struggle onto the cargo ramp; the helicopter is reluctantly held in a hover, her back wheels bouncing along the ground. Moving into her dark shadowed belly, we shove our rifles out the windows and fire into the tree line that hides the dug-in enemy troops. Pieces of aluminum begin to appear on the floor as machine gun rounds rip holes into the fuselage. The chopper begins to lift as the Phantoms make their first run on the tree line, their afterburners adding to the deafening noise. The heat from the napalm fills the helicopter; suddenly ... we are climbing above the inferno. I collapse onto the aluminum floor and try to catch my breath, and staring blankly at the overhead, I am thankful to be alive. The cold wind blasts through the windows and I lay on the floor enjoying it; I open my frayed and torn jungle jacket to help my chest absorb the cool wind. A gunner hands me a candy bar; I am shaking, perhaps laughing wildly, as I tear it from the wrapper and force it down. I am given another but I merely look at it. There is no more room in my stomach, and I decide to eat it later.

The flight to Dong Ha is short; there are no detours. The chopper lands in our company area where we are met by a host of our peers. Stumbling from the cargo ramp, we are told that there is food waiting in the mess hall, and the ravenous team moves as if in a dream following the smell of hot food. Approaching the tin roofed, plywood building that lies hidden beneath layers of sandbags, I feel as though I will collapse and pass out. We attack the food like starved wolves; our eyes, filled with fear, adrenaline and hunger, blaze like embers. We eat standing and after a mere half dozen bites ... I run outside as it all comes back up. I am not alone. None of us can keep the food down. Hunger refuses to leave us; it will take more than these meager offerings to dislodge his claws from our guts, we have moved far beyond that.

I have learned that hunger is more than just being without nourishment, he reaches deep within your soul and ravages all that he finds there. The open wounds that his claws gouge leave deep scars as reminders that he has visited. I will never forget his brief visit and I will never allow him to return—there is no pain that hurts as deep, there is no anguish as not knowing when he will leave. Our team is ordered to stand down, we have been used up … we have nothing left. The reporter has left without saying goodbye. He is on his way to Saigon. I wonder to myself if he will find the pieces of green aluminum that I picked up from the floor of the helicopter and shoved into his shirt pocket; they will make great souvenirs. Silently I wish him well. We grew to like and respect him while he hunted and suffered with our team. Not once did he complain and not once did he demand to be treated any different than the rest of us grunts. Weeks later his story will travel through the AP wire; we will receive copies from home, but sadly … we will never hear from him again.

Now we learn of the carnage. The fighting to the east of our RZ was terrible for the Ninth Marines. They lost an entire rifle company to the 90th NVA Regiment. The battle was fought very close to us and we may have contributed to the ultimate success by destroying some of the enemy reinforcements with artillery; we will never know. To us it was just another bad patrol into the DMZ. We are never told what our efforts may have contributed, there is no time for any of that. For us there is only the next insertion, the next kilometer, the next hill, the next vine, the next canteen of foul,crawling crater water. Many months later we learn that the battle was designated Operation Buffalo; deservedly so, it will create living legends of the brave men of the First Battalion, Ninth Marine Regiment, now known as "The Walking Dead." Our enemy, the 324B NVA Division, left well over 1,300 bodies on the field, but how many did they carry north? How many of those that were carried past us in the dark of night died as they crossed the river into the cauldron of artillery that we brought to bear? Historians will discuss the battle and books will be written, yet few will ever know about the tiny recon team that moved through the tangled inferno, silently hunting and destroying the enemy … while thirst cracked our lips and hunger gnawed into our souls.

5

The Gift

Our team, weak from hunger, is being sent south to China Beach for three days of R&R. The Major, always looking out for his men, wants us on a plane as soon as possible; it is his way of telling us that we have done an exceptional job. We have heard endless stories of the air-conditioned cornucopia that waits within the Freedom Hill PX in Da Nang; it is the reward that bush Marines live for and is much more coveted than any of the scraps of multicolored ribbon that we scorn so openly. Other teams that have received the reward have returned from the south with tales of infinite flavors of ice cream and oceans of crystal clear water that is served in frosty glasses packed with smoking crushed ice; these are the stories that offer hope and promise to those that live under the umbrella of North Vietnamese artillery and rockets, praying each day that they will reach their twentieth birthday.

As we scrub the greasy carbon from our rifles, the Company Gunny enters the sanctity of our lair. He tosses a yellow envelope to the TL; it contains our travel orders. We are told to be at the airstrip the following morning at 0600. Our plywood hooch is alive with noisy excitement; embellished speculation of what we will find to the south gushes from the half starved Marines. The steady buzzing from the hair clippers that offer only the standard, generic, shaved-head haircut mixes with the metallic rattle of automatic weapons being field stripped for cleaning; the constant slamming of the crooked screen door punctuates our ecstatic laughter. The screen door, having been repaired numerous times with the cardboard from C-Ration cartons, remains suspended in a state of torment as the dusty wind attacks the flimsy, ragged portal. The door flies open with each assaulting gust; the piece of scrounged inner tube that once acted as a spring stretches to the exaggerated lengths that long ago stripped the resilience from the rubber. Often the makeshift door has to be coaxed back into a closed position. Above the naked rafters, the tin roof beats like a steel drum as loose sheets of rusty corrugated metal flap wildly in the hot wind; only sandbags and wire anchor the flailing metal, preventing it from being completely ripped loose. The plank floor of our home is littered with used rifle bore patches and C-Ration candy wrappers that dance about as the dusty wind blows through the torn screen walls. Chocolate is being offered to the demon that has chewed into our guts for so long; it is an offering that we hope will coax him to leave. The hair that has been sheared by the buzzing clippers now floats in puddles of spilled gun oil and bore solvent. Piles of jungle utility uniforms, encrusted with the dirt and sweat of our stay in the DMZ, wait to be taken to the elderly Vietnamese laundress that waits patiently just outside the barbed wire perimeter.

I finish cleaning my weapon and, without being asked, gather the bundles of laundry from the others. After wrapping them in a poncho to create a single, manageable package, I give the ragged screen door a hard kick and pull the huge bundle into the tight opening until it is stuck. My peers come to my aid, kicking and pushing the smelly collection until the green plastic slides through. With the huge bundle thrown across a shoulder, I enter into the ominous sea of wire bringing the task that will, hopefully, contribute to filling the woman's modest rice bowl. I move through the tiered rings of concertina and razor wire along the narrow twisting path designed to confuse North Vietnamese sappers; sweating profusely, I pause each time the poncho is snagged. The old woman sends volleys of words in my direction that I do not understand, but from her demeanor I know that they are the words of encouragement. She stands alone in the brutal heat leaning into the dusty wind, her frail body is neatly dressed in tattered but clean pajamas, the deep fluid black eyes that resemble small wells of ink are shaded by her conical rice-straw hat; it is a timeless image that spans centuries. Lacking detergent and machinery, she will pound the grime from the faded uniforms using ancient flat rocks that are scattered along the banks of the Song Mieu Giang. In the past I have left extra piaster notes or chocolate in the pocket of a jungle jacket, hoping the gift will make her life somewhat easier. It is a terrible mistake, as I have been taught nothing about the customs of the country we defend; it is an ancient society that is based on honesty and integrity, where the slightest deviation from etiquette will cause a loss of face. The chocolate may be accepted but money is not an honorable gift. Associated with greed, it does not come from the heart. Each time the worn and wrinkled notes are discovered, they are returned by scarred and gnarled hands that have seen a lifetime of toil, endurance, and terrible suffering. How has such a frail creature survived for so long in such a harsh land where nature and war offer no quarter? For the Vietnamese farmer, life is the cycle of rice crops, wealth is the family, and hope is found in prayer; within the parameters of the ancestral community, time is irrelevant. The old woman emerged from the rich soil of Indochina to travel through a timeless circle provided by nature. With faithful harmony, she meets each trial and obstacle, never questioning, never avoiding, but always accepting. When the circle is completed she will follow the path that a lifetime of enlightenment has prepared that leads to Nirvana.

I worry that the bundle of laundry is too heavy a burden for her tiny body to carry; before I am able to express my concern she opens the green plastic and divides the clothing into two large rice baskets. The baskets are suspended from each end of a hardwood pole that she balances across a calloused, bony shoulder. In her free hand I place a number of chocolate bars; the hand seems so small, so innocent, so inadequate. Her eyes are piercing, yet they are filled with the warmth of sincere compassion, and though very old, seem young, energetic and alive. Beneath the shade of the frayed, conical hat, a red-brown betel stained smile thanks me for the gift; traditionally, she will not keep such a special gift, instead, the chocolate will be placed on the altar of her ancestors. Her culture is about caring, giving, and remembering those who have parted this world. She has no concern for her own comfort, there is only concern for the comfort of her ancestors in the afterlife. Still smiling, she begins the trek to the riverbank; she moves gracefully across the dry, cracked paddies that have been tended by countless generations of her ancestors, soon the drenching rains will arrive and the cycle will begin anew. With no apparent effort she manages the balanced burden; her sandals make slapping sounds as her tiny feet carefully step through the debris of war. Protectively, I watch until she has vanished into the distance. Months later as the monsoon season arrives, she is no longer seen near the wire; her rice bowl is gently placed at the family altar allowing another to take its place—one departs and another arrives, the ageless cycle is everlasting. In the ninth month of the Chinese lunar calendar, the monsoon rains return to Quang Tri province bringing the promise that life will go on. Torrents of rain flood the ancient paddies while toiling water buffalo plow and churn the fresh, rich mud; riding on their massive backs and dwarfed by the lethal curved horns, children coax and soothe the happy beasts with simple music from bamboo flutes. The old woman has returned to the soil of her ancestral home; now she will rest amid the lush brilliant-green rice shoots that promise a bountiful harvest. Her journey is completed.

> *...the buffalo toil,*
> *the bamboo flutes play,*
> *the rain fills the paddy,*
> *the circle continues...*
>
> The author

6

Da Nang

We are flown south aboard a C-130 that is filled to capacity. The dark interior of the huge aircraft is crammed with a vast array of cargo; we find places to sit, squeezed into the tight mazes of boxes, weapons, and sacks of mail. Strapped to the cargo ramp, two dozen or more bloated bags are stacked neatly in a pile that resembles a pyramid; the smell that fills the plane leaves no doubt as to what they contain. The flight is mercifully short.

The Da Nang air base is alive with constant activity. We are told that it is the busiest airport in the world. The noise is a constant, unrelenting attack upon our hearing as fighter-bombers take off and land. The jets sortie in groups, their afterburners blazing with the blue ringed fire that is needed to carry the massive bomb-laden wings to altitude. The thrust from the powerful engines sends waves of violent tremors through the concrete apron that we stand on. Returning fighters with naked wings roll along the runway, their speed is harnessed and dampened by trailing drag-chutes. The concrete airfield seems alien to Vietnam. We are used to obscure, isolated, dust choked airstrips that are covered with steel matting; the Da Nang airport is a marvel of American engineering.

As we wander aimlessly in the direction of the terminal hangar, we have found an old friend. "Spooky," a C-47 gunship that is so dear to Marines, sits peacefully alone on the broiling tarmac. Though we know our old friend well, it is the first time that we have seen the deadly aircraft in daylight. The old plane, dressed in a coat of dark olive green, seems so small, so insignificant, and so vulnerable amid the sleek Phantoms and Skyhawks. We are the living witness to the darker side of "Spooky" and the ruthless carnage that she can bring to bear. Each night, her guns send uninterrupted streams of brilliant orange tracers streaking through the black sky into the enemy below, never pausing, never offering pity; we have been told that as many as six thousand rounds per minute slam into the jungle floor. Like mesmerized children, our group of admirers moves along the olive green fuselage. Occasionally one of us reaches to touch the hot aluminum skin, while excited anecdotes of past encounters with our friend are exchanged; each of us contributes to the remembrance. An Air Force sentry approaches and tells us to move away from our friend. He is dressed in a uniform that seems absurd and comical to our ragged little band of skinny brigands. His starched jungle uniform is pressed with razor-edged creases, the trousers tucked into leather boots shined to a deep gloss; a huge bush hat with one side of the wide brim neatly folded and held in place with a metal snap shades the eyes that are hidden behind gold rimmed aviator sunglasses. Ignoring him, our attention locks onto the weapon that he carries. The rifle has a grenade launcher attached to the underside of the barrel; it is the first weapon of this type that we have seen, we are envious. Though we are dressed in clean utility uniforms and display the Marine parachute insignia that we reserve for special occasions, our appearance is somewhat unkempt in this bastion of starch and polish. Our worn out jungle boots and brilliant golden wings are testament to our identity as well as our mission. The loaded Colt .45 automatic pistols that each of us carries so close, coupled with hungry, blazing, wolf eyes, are confirmation that we truly are a "hunting pack." Although the sentry is merely a harmless showpiece and should not be feared, we retreat and move away from the old plane.

Da Nang, called Tourane by French colonials, has been swept into unbridled capitalism. Continuous, silent streams of bicycle traffic weave through the beautiful shaded boulevards, twisting and merging, never stopping, never pausing. From the flowing silence emerge the gentle sounds of bells that signal to the slower pedestrian traffic; the fused ringing becomes synchronized until the final blended harmony becomes soothing music. As if each bell is an individual instrument, the strengthening concerto floats upwards from the orchestra to where the completed masterpiece is muffled by the flourishing branches of overhanging frangipani trees. The gentle symphony reverberates through the lush trees that shed their fragrant, creamy white and yellow blossoms into the path of the weaving streams. Bicycle tires grind the fallen blossoms into the pavement, creating a slippery carpet of heavy perfume that mixes with the steamy humid air until a thick pungent balm fills our lungs with its sweet, sticky ambiance. The boulevards are lined with shops that have spilled their wares onto the wide sidewalks, making it impossible to walk anywhere but in the slippery street or in the gutters. Merchants sit in the shade sipping *nuoc mia* or perhaps *tra xanh,* while impatient fingers travel with lightning speed across the hardwood beads of a well oiled abacus; the beads have been polished to a deep brown sheen from the accumulation of countless fortunes. The greedy merchants offer inventories stocked with endless quantities of American goods—cigarettes, military uniforms, liquor, boots, candy, soft drinks, beer, soap, toothpaste and countless other items that so abundantly find their way from our supply chain into the black market. The shops are filled with the things that have been sent to us but we shall never see; we are enraged and spew profane insults toward the smiling fat proprietors that offer no compassion to the many blind and crippled beggars crawling along the slippery gutter at their feet. We pass a huge display of American military clothing; stacks of green boot socks tied into neat bundles of three are piled high on the table, a few of the bundles have fallen onto the sidewalk. Taking a bundle from the pile, I examine the lush quality of the thick soles and caress the smooth clean softness; it has been a long time since I was issued new socks. Watching me with eyes filled with frantic greed, the anxious merchant anticipates payment. Looking him in the eye, I speak the words that shatter his shallow, callous world, "you souvenir me"; I stuff the soft, spongy, socks into the cargo pocket of my faded green trousers and with complete disregard for the consequences, I continue on through the falling petals. From behind comes an onslaught of angry voices as a group of assailants approach; quickly, they back away as I lift my jungle jacket to reveal the hidden Colt. I am now a thief; a criminal that has, without fear or conscience, committed armed robbery.

The city is engrossed with the upcoming election; colorful signs inscribed with words that we do not understand advertise the virtues of each candidate. Unable to ask directions, we climb aboard a city bus hoping that it will eventually arrive at China Beach. The crowded interior is filled with wicker baskets of produce and noisy chickens. Toothless peddlers thrust overpriced American soft drinks and beer in our faces while an army of pimps offer the services of young "virgins"; choking exhaust fumes that infiltrate up through the many cracks and holes in the rusted floor adds to the lunacy. An ancient diesel engine billowing a cloud of thick, black, oily smoke violently shakes the old bus as it strains to traverse the short distance from one stop to the next. The glassless windows are covered with thick steel mesh that, hopefully, will prevent grenades from being tossed into the bus from speeding motorbikes. There is no protection from beneath and silently I try to determine the damage that a mine or satchel charge could inflict if thrown under the old, tortured chassis. We have made friends with an Air Force Master Sergeant sitting across the aisle; he tells us that we are invited to their Club. The Master Sergeant, perhaps in his mid-forties, does not resemble a fighting man. Dressed in civilian clothing, his white silk shirt is stretched tight across a bulging stomach, the consequence of prolonged good living. We immediately like our new friend; speaking fluent Vietnamese, he buys each of us a warm beer from one of the many peddlers prowling along the aisle. He tells us that he has been in Vietnam for the past three years and explains the political corruption that accompanies the coming election. He seems very much at home here. From a wallet that he has hidden in his sock emerges a photo of his fiancée; he passes it to us as if seeking our approval. The Vietnamese woman, perhaps half his age, is extremely beautiful. He explains that she is well educated and comes from a very nice family, adding quickly that she is no bargirl. Each of us makes the expected exaggerated sounds of envy and admiration while our new friend carefully gauges the response.

Before he replaces the new photo back into the safe haven of the wallet, he looks at it admiringly, obviously our friend is very proud of his pretty *mademoiselle*. He asks concerned questions about the terrible fighting to the north; it is apparent that he has a warm place in his heart for bush Marines. We are surprised that he has an interest in our little piece of the war and like excited children we bombard the poor man with answers filled with our personal views of the conflict along the DMZ. Like a patient father, he tries to absorb each word from the growing excitement and finally raises his hands to calm us; then, without speaking, he points to the individual that he wishes to answer. Again he invites us to be his guest that evening, and our TL tells him that we have very little money with us, perhaps each man has ten dollars in crumpled notes of Military Payment Certificates. Our new friend laughs as he informs us that Marine money is worthless in their Club; we will be the guests of the U.S. Air Force.

Outside the lurching bus, the vibrant city is coming alive as assorted Japanese motorcycles with American drivers race past the mesh covered windows. Gracefully perched behind the drivers are willowy, raven-haired Vietnamese girls, their silk *Ao Dai* flow and flutter in the wind like the wings of white butterflies. The jovial Master Sergeant gives us thorough directions to the Air Force Staff NCO Club and to the Freedom Hill PX; reaching his stop, he bounds from the bus only to be immediately surrounded by a host of merchants, beggars and prostitutes. A volley of Vietnamese words are sent into the crowd and they flee from the hulking man. The Master Sergeant, older than most of our fathers, has left us in an enthralled state of admiration; for many weeks, he will be the central subject of countless exaggerated tales that are told and re-told as we brag to other recon teams about the adventurer that we encountered in Da Nang. The smoking bus continues along the boulevard in the direction of the Freedom Hill PX; behind us, our new friend disappears into the thick, black, oily fog.

The PX is a huge structure built of wood and resembles the set of a western film; a large sign attached to the front declares that we have reached our reward. From exhaust vents that suck the heat and steam from overworked grills come the rich, greasy aromas of sizzling ground beef smothered in onions and of potatoes frying in deep fat. In order to enter the cool sanctuary, we are told to check our weapons; I will not surrender my pistol and since it is well hidden under my shirt, I swear that I am unarmed. The feast is beyond description; a mixture of grease and condiments stream down my hands and onto my arms as I wolf down the fat-laden hamburger. I am overcome with a surge of indescribable happiness; across the table I see bliss in the eyes of the grenadier as he savors a glass of cold milk. Like ravenous wolves, none of us makes a sound; each man is lost deep within private thoughts while our bodies absorb the food as quickly as it is consumed. Before draining the clear water from a tall, frosty glass, I stare into the frozen prism depths of the crystalline ice shards as if admiring rare diamonds; for the rest of my life a simple drink of clean water will always be very special and can never again be taken for granted.

Silently, I wonder if there are, at this very instant, other Marines somewhere deep in the bush drinking the crawling stagnant slime from craters as worms bore into their guts. How is it possible for two opposite extremes to exist so close, does abundance always lurk so close to destitution? With scanning eyes, I have noticed stares coming from a nearby table; perhaps they find our appreciation of this wonderful feast comical. Their starched shirts, emblazoned with colorful patches, is evidence that these are not combatants but are representative of the thirty or more support troops that are needed to maintain a single bush Marine. Suddenly, I am self-conscious; during the frenzied assault on the food, my dignity has taken a brief sabbatical. Without speaking I look toward the table of critics. Now, the shame has been reversed as each averts his eyes downward staring at the bounty that they take for granted each day. For an instant I consider approaching them to explain our ravenous behavior but quickly realize that it is a saga that they, the fat and protected, cannot comprehend. Perhaps they should be told that in order to obtain the comfortable socks that were to be sent north, I have found and crossed the thin line that separates the virtuous from the felon. Without looking in their direction, I decide that this is not the proper time for an assault on the weaker pack; in revered silence I rejoin my feeding brothers.

59

Eye of the Tiger

We arrive at the R&R Center at China Beach. Other Marines, also fresh from the bush and forward areas, sit in the coarse sand staring eastward, toward the thin line that separates the South China Sea from the cloudless sky. Thousands of miles beyond the horizon, the focus of their quiet thoughts is waiting.

Although cold beer is served in small oceans, there is no boisterous behavior, only the peaceful quiet that lingers as young, tortured minds make futile attempts to understand the insanity of the bush war. Ragged jungle trousers, rolled up to the knees, expose legs that are covered with festering leach bites, white scaly patches of ringworm and the oozing scabs of jungle rot; salty ocean water soaks into the open wounds bringing with it the fire of healing. A lone Marine swims into the placid surf as if attempting to cross the endless miles of shark-infested sea to the Philippine Islands; quickly he returns to his place alongside the others that are now surrounded by growing piles of empty *Biere LaRue* bottles.

We join our comrades at the water's edge and also look toward the haze-gray line; there is no structured conversation, only incomplete sentences that are sparsely laced with the familiar names of distant cauldrons that need no additional explanation ... Ca Lu ... the A Shau Valley ... Hill 881 ... Con Thien ... Elephant Valley ... the Co Bi -Thanh Tan Valley ... the Arizona Territory ... the Hai Lang Forest ... the Da Krong Valley ... the Ba Long Valley ... Khe Sanh ... the Hai Van Pass ... Helicopter Valley ... Mutters Ridge ... the Rockpile and Razorback ... An Hoa ... Pagoda Valley. Though words are seldom exchanged, we acknowledge one another with silent nodding often followed by a profane whisper. Like wolves returning from the hunt, our blazing eyes meet and words are not needed; the rotten boots, infected leech bites and vigilant scanning eyes assure each of us that we are among our own kind.

As the sun begins to set behind Marble Mountain, we search out the old French hotel that houses the Air Force NCO Club. The architecture of the hotel reflects the golden age of French colonialism; the opulent building could easily be from a scene found in Paris or perhaps in the *Vieux Carre* section of New Orleans. Along the sidewalk that surrounds the shaded hotel, South Vietnamese soldiers are posted as sentries. Armed with vintage American weapons, they patrol their charge with an obvious nonchalant attitude. Just inside the wide double doors, a group of graceful Vietnamese hostesses greet us; with broken English we are asked to check our weapons, and again we insist that we are unarmed.

Our jovial friend from the bus calls to us from the top of a stairway. He encourages our shy band to come upstairs and leads us to a huge room that seems to be a combination of lounge and restaurant. From nowhere, bottles of ice-cold beer materialize in our hands; we are not asked to pay. Around us, the dark Club is awash in good living; we stand in a tight group facing outward, as if we are harbored in the bush, our eyes attempting to comprehend this strange world. I am spellbound. The blinding object hanging on the plastered wall captivates my mind as colorful neon patterns flash brilliantly, creating the illusion of a waterfall that frames the logo of a Japanese beer. It is a wonderland of abundance and a refuge from the napalm-charred misery that encroaches so near. Though the night passes much too fast, we savor each precious moment while realizing all too well that this brief interlude is fleeting and may never occur again. With the arrival of the morning sun, we leave the enchantment of the old hotel. Each of us thanks our host; without option, he has assumed the role of father and mentor to our band of teenaged warriors. He looks into the trees, and avoid's our eyes as he tells us to be careful when we return north; he is obviously concerned for our welfare. I remove the Marine Corps parachute insignia from my jacket and hand it to him. He seems honored, and the TL tells our friend that he is now one of us. As we wander aimlessly away from the hotel, I turn to wave farewell; clutching the gold plated insignia, our friend waves until we disappear into the hordes of hustlers and merchants.

We fly north aboard a CH-53; the massive helicopter is filled with fresh fodder to feed the cauldron. In contrast to these Marines who have just arrived in Vietnam, we seem old and hard. Our appearance supplies the fuel to fire their nervous anticipation. I lay prone on the floor of the helicopter staring through the partially opened hatch that the aircrews call the "hellhole"; we fly low along the beach, just above the strong, frothy waves that rush to shore as their windswept crests trail a mist of salty spray. I am joined at the small portal by an eager but bewildered Marine. Subconsciously, I assume the role of tourist guide as I recite the names of the landmarks below. He listens attentively, as the blast of wind that forces its way through the chopper and the deafening noise from the turbines assaults his mind. Each lurch that comes from empty rotors searching for resistance causes him to tighten his grip on the new M-16. Hiding my own anxiety and fear, I tell him not to be concerned. Remembering that it was not so long ago that I was also a stranger to the madness, I try to reassure his fragile confidence.

Dong Ha combat base appears below. From the air it resembles an ill designed garbage dump, where streams of smoke flow across the furnace of naked red earth. Across the barren expanse, helicopters churn hot dust storms that mix with the red clouds created by tank treads and truck tires. My mind, filled with indelible memories, wanders to the cool, fragrant boulevards that meander through Da Nang; perhaps it was all a dream. Were those that we observed lounging beside swimming pools merely apparitions? Was the cool, clear, chlorinated elixir that filled the concrete depths merely an illusion? We have visited the dominion of Bob Hope and Ann Margaret, where the rich aromas of deep fried delicacies mingle with the fragrance of falling petals and where jewel encrusted drinks of water are ignored and wasted. I think of those that are living such lavish lives of luxury and I am filled with envy, yet mysteriously, a small part of myself feels pity for them. Perhaps they will never fully appreciate what they have. Quickly I retrieve my mind from the tangent that it has taken; their war is not my concern, their fate is not my destiny. Close by, the heat and shadows of the Truong Son wait patiently.

7

Ca Lu

We have been sent into the Ca Lu area; the tiny outpost located there plugs the entrance to the Da Krong Valley, the valley that runs south until merging with the A Shau Valley. It is a contested place, strategically located deep within the pass that knifes its way through the Truong Son. Well over seven hundred years have passed since Cham pirates defended this same passage by attacking the Khan's dismounted Mongol invaders, driving them from the region. The ancient trade route that connects the fertile coastal plain of Vietnam to the far inner reaches of Asia begins to the north of Ca Lu and meanders south and west and then north again, severing the very spine of Indochina. The passage twists and turns as it follows a corridor of deep river valleys and treacherous gorges that slice through the craggy jungle-strangled peaks to the triple junction of the Rao Quan, the Da Krong and the Quang Tri rivers. From the star that is formed by the merging rivers, the vast Khe Sanh plateau is traversed for an additional ten miles on to Lao Bao, where the border is crossed into Laos.

The old trade route is as mysterious as it is beautiful and is as deadly as it is majestic; it is where ancient caravans entered the Kingdom of Champa bringing ideas and wealth many centuries before the world knew of either Alexander or Christ. Long before the Vietnamese moved south from southern China sometime around 500 B.C., the Cham had already arrived; their origin is

Beneath the triple canopy near Ca Lu it was "a mushroomed world that has never known the sun."

thought to have been India. The seafaring Cham established coastal strongholds along the southern coastline and from these ports they attacked the fleets of treasure-laden trade ships traveling the ancient sea-lanes that connected India with China. Their kingdom, situated along this crossroad, became a thriving center of culture, inhabited by scholars and artisans from all regions of Asia.

To the north of Champa was Nam Viet, the land of the hated Vietnamese. War-like, ever expanding and always at odds with the Chinese to their north; Nam Viet tried desperately to drive the Cham from a kingdom that stretched south from Indrapura, later known as Da Nang, for some seven hundred kilometers. To the south of Champa lay the true prize, the rich, fertile soil of the Khmer Empire. To the north of Indrapura, where the coastal plain is narrowest, was the three hundred kilometers of battleground that stretched from present day Da Nang to just north of Dong Hoi; though the adversaries were separated by the natural boundary of the Ben Hai River, the entire contested area was claimed by both. The pass at Ca Lu, held by the Cham, was centrally located in the disputed region; Nam Viet recognized the pass as the key to Champa and the lush, fertile riches of the far south.

The Chinese occupied Nam Viet in 111 B.C. and remained until A.D. 938, renaming the region Annam: "the pacified south." During this period the Cham established fortified villages along the caravan trail and kept the Chinese at bay for the entire one thousand years. In A.D. 1000 Mahayana Buddhism found its way into Annam, having traveled across Asia from India; when it found the pass at Lao Bao, Buddhism entered the region and displaced the simple philosophy of Confucianism. Barely ten years later, a Buddhist follower, Ly Thai-to, seized power; the new monarch quickly renamed the land that lay from Da Nang north to the Red River Valley as Vietnam. His dynasty, the Ly, would rule until A.D. 1225. Driven by conquest, the Vietnamese attacked Champa in A.D. 1044 and for over four hundred years they attempted to dislodge the fierce Cham pirates from their coastal kingdom. Midway through the four hundred year war, Kublai Khan invaded Vietnam near the Red River Valley. During the fierce invasion that would ultimately last for over thirty years, the Vietnamese turned their aggression from the Chams to meet the advancing Mongols. With his eyes on the riches of Champa and the Khmer Empire, the Khan sent an entire Mongol army into the pass at Lao Bao. The daring attack, which flanked the Vietnamese, was an attempt to drive the Cham from their coastal bastion and clear the way south to the land of the Khmer. Great battles were fought and it was from the trade villages, established many centuries before, that the Cham launched the attacks that would repel the Khan's invasion and push the remnants of his mauled army back onto the high plateaus of Laos to face the wrath of Siamese warlords.

With the defeat of the Khan, the Vietnamese and Cham

returned once again to their interrupted war. For two hundred years more, the bloody war raged until at last the Chams were defeated and quickly absorbed into Vietnamese society. The Vietnamese, having occupied the Champa Kingdom, then turned their wrath upon the Khmer Empire, pushing them farther into Cambodia, to the sanctuary of Angkor. Then, in the mid–1600s, Vietnam invaded Laos through Lao Bao and stayed for two hundred years, only to be driven back through the pass by the Siamese. In the late 1700s the Catholics arrived and attempted to convert Vietnam to Christianity. The Catholics were hated by the Vietnamese Emperors, and a period of persecution that would last for one hundred years began. Many of the Catholic priests and their followers were imprisoned at Lao Bao; most of these would die from disease, torture, or immolation, and others were beheaded. Midway through the nineteenth century, in the name of the Church, the French arrived in force. Soon, in the high plateaus of the Annam Cordillera they began to grow the finest café in the world and with the French came the poppy and ... Indochina was forever changed. By 1905, engineers were busy constructing the roads that would connect French Indochina with Thailand, Burma, and China. The old caravan trail became Route Colonial 9, the link that connected Laos to the coast and to the railway that paralleled Route Colonial 1—"the Mandarin Road." The wealth that had been stripped from the inner regions of the colony was brought across these new roads to the ships that waited at Haiphong, Da Nang, Vung Tau, Saigon and a host of others; from these ports, café, rubber, tea, pepper, opium, silk, jade, ivory, coal, timber, spices and countless other treasures were shipped to France.

> *You cannot tread the Path*
> *Before you have become that Path yourself....*

Unknown Zen poet

We are to patrol an area some three kilometers from Route 9. It is a very crude road that no longer sees vehicle traffic. Plagued with rockslides and flash floods, it has become a killing zone often lined with company and battalion size ambushes that our enemy maintains. Moving constantly, always illusive, the ambush units have stopped the supply convoys to Khe Sanh; now all supplies are moved west by C-130 or helicopter. We are to search for these enemy units and once the enemy is located, helicopter gun-ships as well as fighter aircraft and Marine grunts will be sent to destroy them. To the east of our patrol area is Nui Ba Ho, the "Mountain of Three Tigers," a steep and lush grotto that forms a razor-edged ridgeline running south to Dong Toan Mountain. One kilometer to our west is Dong Ca Lu, the formidable mountain that dominates the region.

Our eight-man team will move along a rocky streambed for a distance of three kilometers to reach our area of operation. On the map the stream is designated Khe Da Bong, "The Stream of Many Flowers." It is a beautiful area, and from the steep, fern-covered cliffs, small waterfalls cascade to the bamboo choked streams below. White and purple orchids are abundant in the cool mist that the breeze blows from the falling water; at times, colorful rainbows shine in the mist, creating beautiful aurora for the fragile orchids. In the trees, monkeys and birds compete for the food supply; their noise, at times, is deafening.

For this patrol, our TL has been replaced by our platoon Gunnery Sergeant; it is a temporary adjustment until the TL returns. The "Gunny" is a good Marine, but more important, he is a good man. I am once again designated as rear point; I dislike the assignment and would rather be on point or assigned the job of grenadier. Though I often alternate with the "point," for this patrol there will be no rotation; of the two of us he is the better, perhaps he is more cautious than I. He does not have to be here. He left college to become a part of this madness. When the Marine Corps attempted to exploit his education, he protested, writing the letters that would put him into the heat, mud, and rain with us grunts. For this, he has earned an intense respect from those of us that know his story.

We are transported deep into the pass by a heavily armed convoy. The trucks do not stop as we quickly offload and immediately move into the dark jungle; the drivers will continue on for a few hundred meters before turning back. By employing this feint, it is hoped that the enemy will not realize that we have been left behind. As we move rapidly into the thick jungle, we can hear the muffled truck engines strain as the drivers force the tight turns that will change direction and allow escape from the ambush-laden cliffs. Our movement is hurried yet cautious as we work our way toward the six grid squares that we will scour for the next six days. The terrain is very rough and the two new men that have joined our team have trouble moving through the thick rain forest; soon, if they survive, they will also become a part of our "pack" and in turn they will teach those that arrive to replace those that leave. As I slide though the bamboo and vines, I have realized that it is all about the seating aboard an airliner. If you survive the lessons of the bush and you are successful, your reward will be a comfortable seat for the long flight home. If you are a poor student and fail, there is no reward, just an aluminum box in a cold, lonely cargo hold. Yes, it is all about seating and paying attention in class.

We are moving uphill in a southwest direction toward our objective. The point halts the strung-out column and signals for us to take up defensive positions; he has found something and wants to investigate before moving on. The Gunny signals us forward, where we set up a hasty perimeter. I take off my pack and move toward a better vantage point; immediately, I see what the point has found. There has been a recent battle here. The area is littered with ammunition crates, spent rifle and machine gun brass, boots that have been cut from mangled legs and feet, and there are bloody battle dressings, empty plasma bottles and used morphine needles. I move cautiously through the area, the two new men following along behind like a double shadow. Lying near the base of a torn and ripped mahogany tree is a discarded Marine entrenching tool. One of the new men reaches for the folded shovel and I grab his arm; sternly, I warn them both not to touch anything. The enemy will always return to these battle sites to scavenge what the Americans leave behind, they would never overlook something as valuable as an entrenching tool. It may be a trap; I tell my shadows that there may be Chinese Claymores in the trees ready to be detonated by the slightest movement of the shovel. The lesson learned, we move on. I have found a large can of black pepper and I am amazed that the monkeys and rats have not found it. The point comes over to examine my discovery and together we cautiously open the green container. Inside, the pepper is fresh and dry, the pungent aroma makes my mouth water; it is a good find and will be useful.

We move again, the terrain is becoming much more difficult to traverse; it is a steady uphill climb. Dark is upon us and we move into a bamboo thicket to set in for the night. I open a can of chicken and noodles and pour the pepper in until the contents become a thick, gray slush. Now the green can passes to the point and then circumnavigates the perimeter; it is a rare luxury. The black pepper is a possession that belongs to the pack, we will treasure it, and later when the worn can is no longer green and the contents are gone, we will share the memory.

Dawn breaks and we move again, deeper into the Annam Cordillera. We know that our enemy is nearby; we begin to recognize the signs. The enemy is carelessly leaving the clues that advertise his presence. It is a sign that he feels safe here ... confident; there must be a very large unit nearby. As we move, the two new men are having a difficult time. They slip and fall and become entangled in vines. Having to walk backwards, searching for following enemy, I am constantly turning away from my area of responsibility to untangle them from the thorns and vines and my patience wears thin. I want to move at least one of them forward in the column and decide to bring it up with the Gunny when we stop for the night.

We move until dusk and set in for the night. I am too tired to worry about the new men so I decide not to bring the matter up. Darkness comes early under the canopy; without the Gunny speaking, the team automatically goes about the tasks of laying the mines and plotting artillery concentrations. He is the leader and is respected and liked by all, but along with the two new men, he is still an outsider. He gives us our freedom to do our jobs and we recognize and appreciate his knowledge as a leader; he is a bush Marine and he leads from the front, not the rear. In just a few days he and the new men will be accepted into our "hunting pack" that has been together for so long, but until then they must each earn our respect and we must gain their confidence. Today, we have humped hard to cover the last of the three kilometers. The team is exhausted, the Gunny has pushed us to our area of operation. The jungle grows dark, radio watches are assigned and sleep comes swiftly.

Before dawn I wake into a shadowy, mist-shrouded wonderland of Kipling. It is the lair of Shere Khan and I am Mowgli, the "guardian of the jungle." Around me the "gray brothers" are sleeping, resting from the previous day's hunt. In the center of our tiny perimeter, the primary radio operator is finishing his watch. With a small piece of flaming plastic explosive, he heats instant coffee in a discarded C-Ration can; the mist has fogged his Marine Corps–issue glasses that have been taped back together in various places. He looks at me and puts his finger to his lips, wanting me to be still and quiet. Without taking his eyes from the steaming coffee, he slowly points into the trees above us. I look up and see the family of Orangutan perched nonchalantly on the thick limb of a tall mahogany tree. From under the shadow of his worn, floppy, bush hat, the radioman flashes a huge smile; his white teeth blaze beneath the black and green camo paint that covers his face. After a few moments, as if they are bored with us, the family moves away, silently vanishing into the shadows of the canopy. He motions for me to crawl over and together we enjoy the hot coffee and a cigarette. Whispering, he tells me that the family of apes was there when the dawn arrived; he has no idea how long they were watching us in the dark. Together, in the early morning mist of the high jungle, we have enjoyed the surreal vision of the phantom family. To the Vietnamese the Orangutan is Con Duoi Uoi, and to all people of Asia he is known as the "wisdom of the forest."

Joined by one of the new men, the radio operator will never leave Vietnam; forever young, it is their fate, their Karma, their destiny to unite with the other wandering souls in this high grotto. Suddenly, as if a switch is thrown, the jungle wakes from the deep sleep. A chorus of sounds from the throats of birds, tree frogs and monkeys becomes louder and louder until deafening; it is dawn in the Annam Cordillera and time for the "pack of gray brothers" to begin the day's hunt.

We move into our area of operation. The terrain is very rough with steep, rocky, vine-choked streambeds that have cut their way from a high ridgeline above. The Gunny wants to work our way up to the top of the ridge; the point moves slowly and deliberately, negotiating the inhospitable terrain, searching for the ambush that may be prepared by our invisible enemy. This is why he has been chosen to guide us; he is comfortable in his element. The war here is about ambush, and both opponents will play "cat and mouse" for days until the outcome is decided by a fast and furious firefight.

We are moving up a dark streambed toward the top of the ridgeline when three shots from an AK crack just above my head. One round is very close and from the loud report, my hearing is muffled; my inner ear stings, I feel for blood … there is none. The shots came from just a few feet above. The Gunny can see me and looks to see if I am hit. I take one of the eight grenades from my belt and show it to him, he shakes his head … no. I understand if it is thrown and it hits a limb it can roll back into us; I return the frag back into its place. The point is moving up onto the little knoll from where the enemy soldier fired, with the M-16 against his shoulder and with the safety off. He moves like a cat. We follow him and as we reach the top we find three spent, copper colored cartridges lying in a neat little pile. The soldier must have been a sentry and being well disciplined, he allowed us to get within few feet before firing his weapon. Perhaps he fired the rifle only to warn his comrades or perhaps he saw me below and missed with the short burst. We form a hasty ambush and set up the Claymores; I am alone and away from the others, facing the direction that we came from. I hate being back here. It is my responsibility to watch the rear but my instincts tempt me to look toward the rest of the team, I want to share in what they see. The Gunny motions for us to eat and we quietly slip rations from our packs but no one heats them. I have no appetite. My ears are still tingling deep inside from the near miss of the rifle rounds. The Gunny motions again for me to eat; he wants us strong because if attacked, we may have to run for hours to break contact. Above in the trees the canopy has become silent, our enemy is nearby. The monkeys and birds quietly watch this duel just as they watched the Chams and Mongols in another era.

The Gunny has placed his poncho over a low tree limb so that he can get to the rations in his pack. Suddenly, the point is firing a full automatic blast into the jungle below him. His fire is answered with a long burst, its distinct sound identifies the weapon to be an AK; the rounds hit the trees above us. I scan the jungle below searching for a target when the point fires another magazine of twenty rounds on automatic. I do not look in his direction but I hear the muffled metallic sound as he replaces the empty magazine with a fresh one. The jungle becomes silent again. Under the dark canopy, the smells of burned powder and oil smoke from red-hot rifle barrels drift across the little knoll. I have no idea what is going on; I concentrate on my area of responsibility.

The team is falling back toward me when I see movement below; I fire a short automatic burst into the brush. The Gunny moves to me and asks what I saw, I tell him and he lets me know that the point just killed an enemy grunt; he shows me his poncho that has been perforated by the AK burst. He smiles at me and mutters the words "too close." As the team continues to move past my position, the point crawls over and tells me that the camouflaged soldier just walked out of the dark jungle as if looking for us; quickly, he fired twenty rounds into the enemy's chest. The ripped and mangled soldier lay on the ground with his weapon next to him; after the next burst of AK fire came from a few meters away, the weapon vanished. Unable to see who took the rifle, the point sprayed an additional twenty rounds into the thick jungle. The eyes of our friend are blazing white and he breathes rapidly. He has graduated to a higher level in this ambush war; now his bush peers will brag of his deed but he will seldom speak of it again, it is the ancient sign of the true warrior. Though we have killed as a pack in the past, he is the first of our team to kill alone. Others will soon follow him.

The Claymores are collected and we move off of the knoll. There is a streambed that offers good cover so we move to it; we must keep moving. The shadows under the canopy are dancing and we can feel the balmy silence. Now, the new men hinder our movement. They have not learned how to move with stealth, it is their first venture into the bush. Each tiny noise that they make seems to echo through the quiet jungle like an alarm that our enemy will hear. We halt the movement and tell them that if they are not quiet we will all be blown away. They are doing their best, it is not their fault, but there is no time for encouragement. Only abusive threats come from those of us that know the bush. It is not fair but the ambush war is not fair and our threats are much more lenient than the mortars and machine guns that are trying to find us. We are no longer the hunters; having killed the enemy soldier, we have suddenly become the hunted. A green metal tube is passed to me. Inside is the thick, waxy, black and green camouflage paint; one end is green and on the other is black. I smear my face with the black end and then pass it to one of the new men. It will sweat off in a few hours and then it will be applied again. Our survival depends on how fast and how quiet we can move; our only defense against the searching enemy grunts is to find them first. If we can find them, we can bring artillery into the duel and reclaim our place as hunter. The enemy has lost a comrade; their pack will be driven by revenge.

Behind I am seeing fleeting glimpses of movement. I am sure that we are being followed and I pass the word forward. We have found ourselves in a dry streambed that offers very little cover; we cannot stop here, we must keep moving. The Gunny looks back at me and I am looking at movement to my left. He is upset that I am not looking behind. I look toward the back, then I see the movement again. As I am looking he again seems very mad that I am looking to the left. Finally I have had enough and I pass the word up the scattered column that there are enemy to the rear-left and I think that they are trying to envelope us. He nods as if he understands but I have no idea what the new men relayed to him; I am worried. We move out of the streambed and up along a dark, gently sloping ridge that is not as thick as we would like. Suddenly the point halts the column and with a sweep of his arm motions for us to move to our left, on line, up the slope. Searching behind, I think that I see a North Vietnamese pith helmet moving across the far ridge eighty meters away. It is an ambush; from behind they are setting up the crossfire. The point moves us out of the killing zone and we move hard and fast to escape. I have become separated as we move up hill; I must get within the sight of the others so that I am not mistaken for the enemy. Moving fast and feeling totally alone, I come upon one of the new men; he is not looking as I

Summer 1967, Near Ca Lu, moving along the Khe Da Bong, *"the Stream of Many Flowers"*; passing through a very rare opening in the triple canopy we will quickly move back into the dark shadows.

emerge from the thick bush. I chastise him for not challenging me, but then I realize that he has just witnessed his first kill; I pat him on the shoulder and tell him to follow me to the others. The team has moved up and around the concealed ambush and now we are once again the hunters. This is the bush war that all recon teams know so well; a chess match played in a far off land, deep within the most remote region of that land. Dark engulfs the jungle and we squeeze into a defendable harbor site. Throughout the long night we hear movement to within ten meters of our little perimeter. I am sure that it is monkeys or perhaps the family of apes, yet at times the sounds seem human. I cannot sleep, and when it is time for the new men to stand watch I sit with them and comfort each through his baptism into the dark nightmare of this strange, deadly world. Dawn arrives, the jungle comes alive and again we prepare to hunt the enemy.

The Gunny wants to get to the top of the other ridgeline. That is where the main force of the enemy will be found. Our job as recon Marines is to find and observe those units; I am shaking with adrenaline as the team begins to move back down into the streambed. We will cross the rocky killing zone once again and try to work our way up into the lair of the waiting enemy light infantry. At the head of the scattered column, the point crosses the deadly streambed as fast as he can; each man will cross alone. The short time that it takes to traverse the seven meters seems an eternity. I scan the jungle on the other side of the streambed; if the enemy finds where we slept he will follow. My hands are full—I am climbing backwards through the thick bush and trying to help the new man in front of me. When we stop, I wave the Corpsman back to me from his place between the two radio operators. I ask him to take the place of the man in front of me and keep both of the new men together. He agrees and without asking the Gunny we reassemble the column; now, perhaps I will be able to concentrate on my area of responsibility.

We continue our steady movement up the ridge but suddenly the point is changing direction; I hate being back here because information is never passed back and I don't know what is going on. The point has made a sharp turn and he is moving the team back toward the streambed that is now fifty meters below. As he passes near me, I shrug my shoulders and he moves closer and whispers the dreaded words ... "dinks up there." I now know all that I need to know, above us, he has spotted a dug in enemy force. We move along the streambed but the direction seems wrong, my compass indicates that we are moving northeast, back toward Route 9. We have located the enemy base camp and it is time to leave the area. Now my job becomes more difficult; the enemy may follow to ensure themselves that we leave the area. On rare occasions they will notify their sentries to allow us to pass unmolested, thinking that we have not found them; if we are leaving, and have not discovered their lair, we are no longer a threat to them. They know that the information a recon team gathers can be deadly. But, this is not one of those rare occasions. We have killed one of their pack, and possibly more, we have discovered their presence. They will notify the units along our escape route to locate and to destroy our small band. Aware of this, we move hard and fast toward Route 9. Dark is once again approaching and we need water. It is decided to move to the stream below and fill one canteen per man. At the stream, we form a very loose perimeter. I wade into the icy water to provide security for the two new men as they begin to fill the eight canteens. I have spotted something in the flowing water a few meters away and as I move toward it I see that it is a green cloth strap snagged on a rock. At closer inspection I see that the strap is attached to a half submerged enemy canteen. The top is unscrewed, yet it has not had time to fill and sink. I move fast to the new men and tell them to back out of the streambed. Fumbling with the green plastic quart bottles, they move like frightened deer. The Gunny asks what is going on and I tell him about my find. We form the column and move away from the stream, we have surprised an enemy soldier as he filled his canteen; dark is approaching fast. We continue to move toward the road well into dusk and when we do stop, there is none of the usual smiling and whispered horseplay. The Gunny boxes us in with artillery concentrations; none of us will sleep throughout the long, dark night.

We are moving well before dawn. The rising sun sends streaks of light through the canopy above; we are moving through a bamboo wonderland of brilliant golden rays. There will be no stopping until we reach the road. We will eat as we move, it is a difficult day. The new men have become more confident and they are adapting. The Corpsman shows more patience with them than I did; they are finding their places in the team.

We have covered the distance to Route 9 at a very fast pace. The road is nearby but we change directions often to confuse the following enemy. They are following us; though I cannot see them I know that they are there in the dark shadows. We must not allow them to place their ambush along our path. My eyes ache from the constant strain of searching through the layers of jungle. We must be careful not to lead the enemy to the trucks that will extract us; it is a prize that the enemy machine gunners dream of. The point moves through the thickest brush that he can find; we are well hidden. The stands of giant bamboo reach far into the canopy above;

their brown, gold, and green stalks are impossible to move through, yet we are able to follow the extremely narrow paths created by small animals. Some of the stalks are at least one foot in diameter; in my mind I try to calculate whether or not the thick bamboo could deflect an AK round. The point snakes the column through the winding corridors until we emerge from the high wall of thick jungle that lines both sides of the primitive road. The sudden onslaught of unfiltered sunlight blinds us; we have been under the dark canopy for days. We move north along the extreme edge of Route 9 as the radioman asks for the position of the trucks, then he announces softly that we must move another four hundred meters to reach them. We retreat back into the dark jungle and continue our move to the north.

The waiting trucks are located and after notifying them that we are near, we once again emerge onto the road. The brave truck drivers and small security force are happy that we have arrived and are impatient to flee the pass as quickly as possible; the enemy is prowling the high jungle ridges that line both sides of the old road. After climbing aboard the trucks, we speed from the area, the .50-caliber and M-60 machine gunners constantly scanning the ridges. We have done our job. We have found and fixed the sizable enemy unit that is operating nearby. Now, Marine grunts may be sent into the area to destroy them or perhaps Phantoms will attack from offshore carriers or the airbases at Da Nang and Chu Lai. The "cat and mouse" game is completed and we have escaped unharmed, but this is but one game in many. Now the enemy pack will lick their wounds and in the dark shadows of the Truong Son they will prepare for our next meeting.

8

Con Ho

We are deep within the rainforest that chokes the Da Krong Valley. Our eight-man team has formed a very tight three hundred and sixty degree perimeter near a rocky stream, which is in fact the Da Krong River; it is the dry season and the river is now more rock than water. The huge, fully exposed, gray boulders that are strewn through the riverbed create raging rapids during the rainy season. Thick bright-green moss covers the upper half of each boulder, providing an abrupt contrast to the dense golden bamboo that lines the riverbanks; the definite line separating green moss and gray rock, well above my head, marks the depth that the now lethargic river achieved during the past monsoon season.

The heat has become much too severe to continue moving, so we will rest and wait for late afternoon to carry on our hunt. The TL has picked a good location; through a natural tunnel that permeates the thick bamboo, a few meters to our immediate north, the river can be observed. Our vantage point is lethal—the excellent view allows us to direct artillery along either bank. The Claymores are placed along the narrow animal trail that we followed through the impenetrable thicket to enter this isolated bamboo cavern; in order to find us, the enemy must travel the same path. Beneath the canopy it is dark, humid, and hot; black clouds of mosquitoes have found our refuge and are arriving in noisy swarms. The jungle floor is damp and spongy; the scent of decaying vegetation and mushrooms seems to enhance the humidity. Each man lies prone, facing out-ward into the blind of bamboo. Our trap is set, we wait and listen. From the center of the small perimeter drift whispered voices as our situation report and pre-determined artillery concentrations are sent to the anxious relay.

The TL tells me to move alone down to the riverbed. I am to establish a listening post that will eliminate a blind spot. I don't mind the lonely assignment because the leeches have appeared in force; perhaps they are not as bad down there. Leaving my pack within the perimeter, I take only my weapon and ammo belt. It is not far to the river, perhaps eighty meters, yet the thick bamboo is difficult to move through. Unable to see, I move blindly through the wide, smooth stalks, following the peaceful sounds coming from the slow moving water below. The thick bamboo stops suddenly at the edge of the riverbed, forming thick walls that line both banks; the huge gray boulders offer excellent concealment as well as pro-tection from rifle fire. Dropping to one knee, I wait at the very edge of the bamboo, hiding, watching ... listening; when I am convinced that no enemy soldiers are near, I move fully exposed along the wall to a group of large, glass-smooth boulders. A cool breeze is drift-ing down the rock-strewn riverbed. I breathe the cool fresh air deep into my lungs and enjoy the fragrance of the ferns that have min-gled with it. Wading into the shallow water, I find a flat rock and slowly sit down, my eyes constantly searching. The river moves slowly and swirls lazily, bringing the smells of perfumed wood and wild fruit. The cool water feels good as it flows through my worn out jungle boots. From my rock, the riverbed is exposed for one hundred meters in either direction; I have picked a good ambush and the mosquitoes are not as numerous in the breeze. Occasion-ally I glance toward the hidden team; though I am merely one hun-dred meters from them, the distance seems much greater. When placed in a listening post you do not move around. I will not return to the perimeter until someone comes to retrieve me. Things can go wrong; in this thick bamboo you can easily be blown away by your own men. It is best to sit tight and wait.

It is now late afternoon and I know that we will soon move to a night position, hunting along the way. I have rolled down my jacket sleeves because I have become chilled from the flowing water. Sitting cross-legged, I have my weapon in my lap pointed toward the opposite riverbank; I feel as though I am being watched. Though it is a familiar feeling that often proves to be true, I am probably just anxious to rejoin the others. When separated from a recon team, you are as far into the bush as you can possibly venture. You are completely alone; there are no Marines watching your back, your head moves constantly as if on a swivel. Though the bamboo behind me creates an almost impassable wall, I feel very vulnerable.

I hear things ... yet the jungle has become very quiet. The breeze that I enjoyed earlier has stopped and the humid balm of the bamboo thicket has again infiltrated the riverbed, overpowering the pleasant smells that travel with the flowing water. In the quiet, I hear the clear water as it trickles and drips through the rocks; the steady hum of mosquitoes becomes annoying as I strain to hear into the shadowed depths beneath the canopy. I watch the far bank, my eyes constantly searching along the wall of golden-green stalks. My teeth are clenched so tight that the muscles in my jaw begin to hurt; I am no longer the hunter, I have become the hunted. High in the trees, the monkeys have stopped moving and the birds no longer sing; my eyes scan harder now, searching for the enemy that has announced his presence with overwhelming quiet. I remove my bush hat and stuff it into the cargo pocket on my trouser leg. The selector on my M-14 is set to full automatic, my finger presses impatiently against the safety. The mosquitoes have left me; maybe they have found a much larger source of food, perhaps a roving enemy recon team. Now I hear only the water as it moves softly through the rocks that have been polished like glass from the rain of a thousand monsoon seasons ... it as deep as you can possibly get into "the Nam."

I turn to look toward the bamboo wall behind me and see the tiger. He is perhaps fifteen feet away, staring at me through a small opening in the wall. The tiger looks like a painting that has been framed in bamboo. The adrenaline flows hard and fast ... I feel light-headed. The tiger is massive and beyond description; he watches me, his eyes never leaving mine. Motionless, he seems frozen. The black stripes that cross the golden coat blend into the shadows of the bamboo thicket; it is perfect camouflage. He is Con Ho, the master of ambush; having entered his dominion, I now fully understand the meaning of royalty. I feel as though he is looking past my eyes and deep into my soul. Perhaps he knows my thoughts. My rifle is pointed the wrong way; do I dare move it? We watch each other for what seems an eternity. With his constant stare I feel helpless and insignificant. Except for the water that moves through the rocks, the world is silent; only the tiger and I exist.

Slowly I turn the rifle toward him, I realize that I must not fire unless he attacks, our hidden position must not be compromised by rifle fire. The tiger has not moved, his yellow eyes have not blinked; he continues to stare. Perhaps his lair is nearby, safely hidden within the shadows that dance beneath the dark canopy. He has a good supply of water and is probably able to find abundant food along the riverbed. We have heard the stories of Marines dragged from their fighting holes never to be seen again; whether truth or fabrication, I now realize that the stories are possible. Like the fleeting wind, Con Ho can go where he pleases, appearing and disappearing like the souls that wander through the Truong Son. The tiger is motionless. Suddenly, a white tufted ear flinches and a cloud of mosquitoes flees his face.

I glance quickly toward the opposite bank of the riverbed to make sure that no enemy soldiers are watching the encounter. It is just a quick glance, taking only seconds, yet when I turn back the tiger is gone. I have heard nothing and it was so quick. He has simply vanished. Perhaps he has moved to a better vantage point to kill and drag me away. In the thick bamboo he is invisible; his camouflage allows him to creep within an arm's reach, I stare into the wall, waiting for the assault that never comes.

I do not want to be alone with the tiger lurking so near; taking a chance, I leave my post and move toward the hidden team. I move through the thick bamboo, trying to avoid the animal path that I followed to the riverbed earlier. Our Claymore mines have been positioned along the path ready to shred anything that approaches the bamboo cavern. As I approach the team I whisper as loud as possible for them to hold their fire; I search through the stalks ahead for my comrades while nervously glancing behind for the tiger that may be following. We have a password; in reality it is the number seven. If I am challenged with the number three, I better respond with four, if they challenge with five, I better come back with two, and so forth. The number changes daily, so it is important to pay attention. As I approach the perimeter I am not challenged but as I force my way through the entangled stalks and into the cavern, there are rifles pointed at me. The team leader, annoyed at my sudden intrusion, asks in a whisper why I have left my post. The bamboo has torn my clothing and inflicted painful scratches across my face, I am in no mood to be chastised. I drain the water from a canteen; between gulps, all that I am able to say is … "a tiger … a tiger." The rifles quickly point the other way, each man scanning his area of responsibility. I tell the TL that I am not going back down there regardless of what he says, he can go himself if he wants. He and the rest of the team can't stop laughing.

I have looked deep into the eye of the tiger. Now much older,

Da Krong Valley. Con Ho (the tiger) was encountered near this spot. The valley runs south until it blends with the A Shau Valley.

I realize that I witnessed the true definition of majesty ... and majesty is Con Ho; he is the silent lord that prowls beneath the canopy. It is his place, his heritage, his Karma and his destiny, perhaps what the Vietnamese call one's *So Menh* or fate. I was the intruder, the uninvited, and the weak. Why was I allowed to sit undisturbed in the grotto and share his ambush? Did I spoil his hunt with my clumsy arrogance, or did he respect my stealth and patience? Did he know me from some past era that is found across an ocean of time? Did he know me as a reincarnate brother, or perhaps recognize a lost friend from long ago? Perhaps he is the *Bodhisattva*, and having rejected Nirvana, he seeks those of us with impure thoughts, bringing them the gift of enlightenment. Has he also approached my enemy?

Deep within the tiger's eye there is no cunning, nor cowardice; there is no cruelty, nor vice. It is the place where knowledge and truth dwell. It is where honesty thrives and where deceit will never enter. It is where we are stripped bare to face our primeval fears and if allowed, emerge reborn. I have ventured into the Annam Cordillera where I looked into the eye of my protector; he will be with me always....

When the stars threw down their spears,
And water'd heaven with their tears,
Did He smile His work to see?
Did He who made the lamb make thee?
Tyger! Tyger! Burning bright
In the forests of the night,
What immortal hand or eye
Could frame thy fearful symmetry?

William Blake

Many years later, I will tell this story to an elderly Hindu man as we enjoy coffee and conversation. As I told the man of my encounter, a smile came to his wrinkled face and his black eyes suddenly came alive with the fire of youth. Then, when I had finished with the story, he seemed to drift deep into thought as if searching for the answer to a riddle. Only when satisfied that he was armed with the proper words did he offer the explanation that I was blessed and that the tiger will always be my guardian. As we finished the coffee, he stood and with his hands clasped, he bowed slightly at the waist and spoke beautiful words from a storybook culture of far away; when I returned the bow, he politely asked to shake my hand for luck. As he disappeared into a mass of humanity, a sad homesick feeling came over me. I thought of days gone by as my mind drifted back to the fragrant grotto and the friend that briefly shared his world with me.

9

The River

The rains have arrived. Though it is only September, the monsoon season is arriving early in Northern I Corps. It has been raining for over a week with few pauses. The peaceful mountain streams are now raging torrents and the beautiful scenic rivers are now powerful floods.

The clear sky that once tortured us with searing sun is now overcast. The blue has been replaced with streaks of steel gray and black. The dark clouds dip to the earth like molten lava and as they blow past, entire mountains disappear from view. The rain is a constant drizzle that is punctuated with violent downpours. We are not used to the cool weather and we shiver from being constantly wet. The jungle has become a quagmire of mud and leeches; it is impossible to stay dry, everything is soaked. We curse the mud and the rain but the Vietnamese celebrate. Rain is survival for them; their culture is based on it. If the rains do not come the rice paddies will not flood and there will be no crop. The rain is also the ally of our enemy. He will use the clouds to conceal the infiltration of his regiments through the mountains from Laos and from the north through the DMZ. The Third Marine Division will depend on its recon teams much more now and we will fill the void left by observation aircraft that are now grounded due to the weather.

Our team is trucked to an area west of Cam Lo along Route 9. The patrol order states that we are to cross the Cam Lo River by rubber boat and climb the steep banks to the summit of Dong Ma Mountain. Then we will patrol along the saddle that connects Dong Ma to Dong Ha Mountain. Although on our map the distance is only two kilometers to the summit, it is extremely steep with poor footing due to the mud. After five or six days of patrolling the area, we are to establish an LZ and if the weather clears, another team, inserted by helicopter, will relieve us. Our interpretation of the order is, if we have to depend on an extraction by chopper, we should carry all of the rations we can because we are going to be up there for a very long time. It is going to be a wet, miserable, cold and hungry patrol.

We arrive at the designated crossing place, which is about seven kilometers west of Cam Lo Village and about six kilometers east of the Rockpile. Along with our team, the trucks are loaded with a security force of about twelve heavily armed Marines. The boat will hold six men so it is decided to divide our eight-man team into two sections that will cross independently. Our regular point man is sick, possible malaria; I am moved from rear point to the point position. I will cross in the first load, as will the team leader, the primary radio operator and the rear point. The second crossing will bring the assistant team leader, the grenadier, the secondary radio operator and the Corpsman. Two Sergeants are assigned to handle the boat. One will operate the small outboard motor and the other will act as a swimmer in case the need arises to swim with a rope or rescue one of us. The inflatable boat seems no match for the raging water. In the past, we have used these boats to come ashore from submarines, through heavy surf, to perform beach reconnaissance; we have trained endlessly with the black rubber boats. The rain is gushing out of the mountains at lightning speed; it seems that we are trying to cross a flash flood. One of the truck drivers has tied a nylon line to the bow of the boat and connects it to the bumper of a 6x6 truck. If trouble arises, they can back the truck up and pull the boat back to shore.

We climb into the boat and begin the trip across; the tiny outboard motor is struggling against the swift current. Trees are passing us just under the surface on their way to the sea. As spray covers the boat and her occupants, the wet, black rubber shines like polished ebony. Sharp points of broken tree branches, resembling primitive spears, break the surface of the river and create dangerous snags, threatening to puncture the air-filled bladders of the boat. Our objective, the opposite riverbank, is a sheer wall of thick vine-choked jungle; it will be difficult to climb from the boat onto the nearly vertical wall. The deep, strong, earthy smell of the thick rain-saturated jungle is consuming. It smells fresh and lush; I have never seen the jungle so green. There are no monkeys or birds that we usually see. Only Marines have ventured out into this weather.

Suddenly, the bow of the boat begins to lift from the water. Rising and jerking violently, it climbs higher and begins to capsize. The TL is thrown past me, the boat groans as the wet rubber is folded back onto itself; men and equipment are thrown into the powerful current. We capsize and the river has us; the boat covers me and blocks the sun, I struggle to escape the rubber tomb. I grab and claw at the slippery rubber until I see the light of the surface; I am clear. Immediately, I see the Sergeant that is assigned as swimmer, he reaches for me as he removes the rain pants that he is wearing. I grab his arm and hold with all my strength. The rain suit that he is wearing is bibbed with suspenders. He has worn the extra large, baggy suit in case the need arises for him to rescue one of us; he will be able to get out of it fast. My hand slips from his arm and I grab the elastic suspender strap of the rain suit; the strap stretches as the violent river tries to separate us. I hold tight. I will hold him until he is free but then I realize that he is struggling; through choked gasps as the river enters his mouth he tells me that he cannot free the legs of the rain pants. I have him by the strap with my left hand while my right hand is grasping the safety line on the boat; I cannot let go of the boat to help him. The Sergeant seems calm and I am sure that he will soon be free, but the current is too strong and I am unable to hold on. I grip the strap until my hand begins to cramp. He looks at me; his eyes are filled with a mixture of calm and remorse. He tells me to let go of him and use both hands to hang onto the boat. I refuse, and again he tells me to do it. He grabs my hand and tears it from the strap and pushes me away; he knows that he will die. He will not take me with him; then, suddenly, he is swept under. I let go of the boat and try to reach for him ... he is gone. The river has me by the throat and pulls me to the bottom. I am swept through the snags and rocks of the riverbed, tumbling and bouncing along through the cold current until the small amount of air in my inflatable life jacket brings me back to the surface. We are all swept downstream. The river sweeps me into a raft of trees that are trapped against the bank. I hold on to the slippery tree branches but the river is pushing and pulling me under the raft. The water forces its way down my throat and it comes back up, strangling me as it goes into my windpipe. I hear a voice telling me to grab the rifle, as I turn I see that it is the Company Gunny. He has an M-14 and is pushing the stock at me; I grab blindly for the sling and he pulls me from the river. Safe on the bank, I lay in the mud fighting back the nausea as it rises in my throat. The Gunny is yelling at me wanting to know where the Sergeant is; they are close friends. I roll over in the soft mud and tell him how the Sergeant pushed me away and went under; I could do nothing for him. The Gunny forces me on my feet and we begin to search through the trapped trees. Climbing out onto the raft, I double over as the river water gushes from my guts. Our efforts are futile; the raft of trees and snags is too thick to search through. The Gunny pulls me from the raft and we continue to search down the river; we resemble a hunter and his dog. I am out front as he comes behind pushing me on.

Suddenly he stops and hangs his head. The reality that his friend is gone is setting in. He stares at the river and seems filled with both disbelief and frustration. I walk back to him and take the rifle from his grasp; he does not look at me as I take his arm and guide him back toward the others. Before we reach the trucks, he makes me stop and after taking a few deep breaths the fire returns to his eyes; he begins to bark the gruff orders and once again resumes his role as enforcer. He has placed the grief into a compartment and will deal with it later; the ignorant will consider him cold and hard.

We truck down river to the Cam Lo Bridge; if the Sergeant has drowned he will appear here. The river is strung with razor wire to prevent enemy sappers from approaching the bridge pilings with demolition charges. The Sergeant does not come to his waiting friends. We are standing on the bridge shivering in the drizzling rain; my body aches from being swept through the submerged trees and boulders. It is hopeless; we have lost one of our very best leaders and a good friend. He will be found a few days later, his body entangled in the razor wire. It is a hard loss for us. Everyone liked the Sergeant and wants a share of the blame. I blame myself for not doing more, perhaps I could have done something ... maybe ... if ... perhaps ... what if ... why? Reluctantly, we climb back into the trucks and begin the long, sad trip back to our base at Dong Ha. Though the truck is filled with the voiced opinions from newly arrived replacements, no one from our seasoned team will speak the entire way. We look at each other and words are not needed, we converse with the body language and expressions that are used during long, silent patrols into the bush.

The pack has returned to its lair. After climbing into dry clothes, we are told to draw new equipment and weapons to replace what the river took. I am forcing Silver Fox whiskey down my raw throat to fight the chill of the river when the word arrives that we will be trucked to the Charlie Two Firebase the following morning. We will reach Dong Ma Mountain by foot; a distance of fourteen kilometers across the map, this will be a very difficult patrol. That night, wrapped in my poncho liner, I think about the Sergeant and I see his eyes, they stare deep into my soul from beneath the surface of the black river ... his arms reaching up to me. Then I think about the Gunny; I will never betray his trust. His moment of sorrow and weakness is safe with me. I have learned that under the tough outer shell, he is no different than the rest of us; we are all vulnerable. Staring into the black of night, I listen to the rain pound the rusting corrugated tin roof and wait for the rotgut Vietnamese whiskey to put me to sleep.

10

The Rain

As far as we know, the fourteen kilometers that must be traversed in order to reach our recon zone will be one of the longest humps that any of our teams has ever made. It is still raining; we have been told that a typhoon is to the south somewhere. The four members of our team that were aboard the rubber boat during the failed river crossing have drawn new weapons and gear to replace what was lost in the river the day before. We are issued the newest model of M-16 rifle that will be supplied to the entire unit soon. It has a slower rate of automatic fire and a noticeably different flash suppressor on the muzzle. I like the new weapon because the older model with the split suppressor would sometimes hang on the vines. I take my new friend down to the test fire pit and burn four fast magazines through the tight action; there are no stoppages, it feels and responds like a sound weapon.

We pack as many cans of rations as possible because we will be out for at least seven days. The constant rain is allowing us to carry less water; I decide to bring only four canteens rather than my customary eight. Normally, as now, three of the one-quart canteens will be attached to the back of my ammo belt; the remaining five are usually packed into the outer pockets of my pack. Trimming the weight of four quarts of water from the overburdened pack will be a welcomed change. The reduction in water will allow for the added weight of the extra rations that I have packed. Every item is carefully placed into small waterproof bags; matches, heat tabs, cigarettes, powdered coffee, powdered cocoa, sugar, malaria pills, toilet paper. On my ammo belt, packed into four magazine pouches are the customary twenty rifle magazines that I always carry, each is loaded with eighteen rounds of 5.56mm; two fragmentation grenades are attached to each of the four pouches. Wide, padded belt suspenders are used to support the heavy ammo belt and taped to the left strap is a cylindrical yellow smoke grenade; it is most often used to mark an LZ during extraction. Beneath the heavy ammo belt, worn low on a canvas strap, hangs my Ka-Bar knife. The leather handled fighting-utility knife was designed specifically for the Marines in 1942; when the seven-inch carbon blade is honed to a razor-edge, it can be used for countless tasks. A magnetic compass hangs from my neck attached to a green nylon lanyard. Though the Ka-Bar knife is the icon of all recon units, the compass is the true essence of our mission. It is said that a recon Marine is never unarmed if he carries a compass, the destruction and death that may be summoned with the tiny instrument is unimaginable. The Colt .45 A-1 that I treasure is worn in a shoulder holster under the jungle jacket; a host of seven round magazines are packed in a breast pocket. With the thick leather holster worn against my bare skin, the pistol absorbs the heat from my body and becomes a part of me; the close presence of the hidden weapon is comforting and reassuring. In the bush, to survive and to accomplish our mission, we must move with both speed and silence; equipment must be packed with the utmost care. There can be no noise; the slightest infraction of this basic rule can and will alert the enemy that searches for our tiny band. Each of us, donning our heavy equipment, jumps up and down listening attentively for the slightest sound; there can be no exception. What may be considered an insignificant rattle will become amplified in the silent bush. Like meticulous spiders, we pack and re-pack until we have reached perfection; no detail can be overlooked, nothing can be left behind. I miss my old pack that is somewhere in the Cam Lo River; after months in the bush, a pack begins to fit and the seventy-five pounds of weight we carry becomes a more manageable burden.

We are trucked up to the C-2 firebase and as we cross the narrow, French built Cam Lo Bridge, we all glance toward the direction from where the Sergeant's body will come with the current. Everyone is quiet as we cross the swollen river. I force myself not to look at the razor wire that is strung from bank to bank. I am afraid that I may see his body. Once across, the truck becomes lively and once again there is the exaggerated laughter that masks deep pain. Insults are hurled at one another and we curse the rain and mud. The grunts that are guarding the bridge throw mud at our trucks; stripped to the waist, they run and slide in the slick, red ooze. We have nothing to throw back so one of our men drops his trousers and "moons" them. He is immediately bombarded with red mud that sticks to his butt and covers the rest of us. The truck continues on, at times the huge tires slide through the red slime toward the sloping road shoulder; the grunts chase the truck for a short distance sending volleys of mud into us, until one by one they resume their attacks on one another.

The "Charlie-2" firebase is a quagmire of mud. The underground bunkers are flooded and everywhere there are Marines digging ditches in an attempt to drain the base. It seems like an impossible task. Just up the road a few kilometers, artillery and mortars from the north are mauling the outpost at Con Thien. We want to get out of the muddy firebase as quickly as possible before incoming rockets or artillery arrive. Another of our Force Recon teams is working to the north of the route that we will take and a team from Battalion Recon will be below us to the south. We will pass near their recon zones and it is very important to coordinate our movement with them. The team leader returns from the command bunker; after forming our column, we move along the twisting footpath, traversing the maze of barbed wire that encircles the outpost. Occasionally, as if to amuse myself, I kick at the wire to hear the metallic clatter of empty ration cans; in the dark of night, the slightest movement of the wire will raise a rattling chorus from the cans, alerting the vigilant and anxious machine gun crews.

Our packs have soaked up extra weight from rain and mud. Already drenched to the skin with the red slime, we know that it will be a miserable patrol. We have an estimated fourteen kilometers to travel through rough, flooded terrain just to reach our RZ. In reality, the distance is much more than that due to the rugged topography of the hills and mountains. Our regular point man is gone to Cam Ranh Bay, he has malaria; we will miss our good friend and with his absence, the team seems flat. I am now permanently assigned the duties of team point. Leaving the wire, we pass through a number of flooded fighting holes that are being used as listening posts. The Marines that man the holes look like shivering rats that have been drowned in red slime; with a deep respect, we pass silently through their position. It is true; there is always someone somewhere that is much worse off. No one suffers like our grunt brothers—their terrible plight is legendary among all recon units. There are no better people and there is no finer fighting force in the world. Though everyone is much too miserable to speak, each of us exchanges mud splattered grins that are accompanied by an occasional shaking head. It is as if only those of us trapped in this sea of mud and rain are privileged to share the secret answer to a humorous, complex riddle. The poor grunts, suffering from exposure, patiently wait to be relieved so they can return to their flooded bunkers; they will merely swap one muddy hole for another.

We move all day trying to make as good of time as possible At dark we set in near an abandoned village that is just to the south of us. It begins to rain harder and after the watches are assigned, we roll into our wet, muddy ponchos and try to sleep. The night is long and when my turn for watch comes, I am happy to get out of the flooded plastic sheet and stand up. Torrents of rain and wind are pounding us; there is no escape, no shelter. The TL whispers for me to come over to him. He has a cigarette well hidden beneath his poncho. I stick my head under and take a deep drag … it warms me. Though it is against every rule of combat to smoke at night, this is a rare exception. We are barely able to see one another in the driving rain; the enemy will never see a cigarette that is hidden under the mud-caked poncho. The rain comes in sheets all through the night and when I am relieved I remain standing with the Marine that has relieved me. Soon we realize that nearly the entire team is standing to escape the flooded ground. As the rain intensifies, I surrender to the cold deluge; wrapping myself into the wet, muddy plastic, I try to sleep.

Before daylight, I wake shivering and half submerged in a deep puddle of cold rainwater, the edges of my poncho floating beside me. I pray that I am dreaming. Leeches cover my legs, their bodies filled to the point of bursting, gorged with type "O" Positive. The crotch of my jungle trousers is caked with blood; a leech has fed on my groin. My wrinkled fingers struggle with the bottle of insect repellant and as I squirt it on their membrane-like skin, I vent my rage on them with frantic curses that are filled with disgust. As I watch them fall off in agony, I scratch at the wounds to maintain the flow of rich, clean blood that will hopefully prevent infection; the repellent burns deep into each wound. Shivering furiously as I try to light a smoke, I wish that we could find a shelter from the driving rain, if only for a few moments. The constant pounding has made my head and shoulders sore. I want to start moving so that I can warm up. My body aches from the beating it took in the river and the hard hump the day before; we have had very little sleep. The TL passes me a bottle of cough medicine and I take a deep drink. It burns into my empty stomach, where it begins to radiate heat through my body; I pass it on to the next man. We have to move with stealth and coughing can give our position away. The ATL has a piece of C-4 burning that heats a can of cocoa; it smells wonderful and he passes it around, it goes well with the cough medicine. I don't want to let go of the warm can; it feels good on my shriveled fingers. Passing it on, I light another cigarette, I manage only two deep drags before the rain soaks the thin paper and it disintegrates. In slow motion, I stand and put on my waterlogged gear. My new pack has picked up too much weight from the rain, so I decide to dump a canteen. I punch holes in the plastic with my Ka-Bar and bury it in the mud. I now have only the three canteens left on my belt; in this rain I am sure that it is an ample amount. I look at my compass. The TL comes up and we compare the map, which is wrapped in a piece of clear plastic, with the terrain. Without speaking, we agree that we will follow a course that will force us to move through a deep valley; it will take until at least midday to cross the planned route. I squirt insect repellent on my soaked clothes in hopes of keeping leeches off, but know that it is a futile effort. The TL and I have been together since boot camp, we know each other well. He looks at me and asks if he looks as bad as I do; I tell him that he looks like hell … we are bush Marines … we have learned to endure and to accept. It is still dark under the thin jungle canopy and the rain continues. As I begin the day's hump, I curse Vietnam, I curse the Marine Corps and most of all I curse myself for being in this wretched situation.

In the jungle, moving downhill can often be as tough as moving uphill. As we move toward the bottom of the valley, we use the vines and trees to prevent sliding to the bottom. The mud is very loose and it is difficult to remain upright. At times I sit down and let myself slide from tree to tree. The going is much tougher than we had expected. We reach the floor of the valley at midday; our estimated time of arrival to the next peak is no longer realistic. The floor of the valley is choked with tall, wet elephant grass; it has provided a perfect ambush site for black clouds of mosquitoes that compete with the leeches for our blood. Now we are hoping that the rain will fall harder to drive them away. I quicken the pace; we have to get across this valley. We are exposed to the enemy forward observers that constantly search for targets of opportunity. From their hidden bunkers, they can bring artillery to bear from nearby North Vietnam. Silently, I wonder if it is possible to be drained of blood by mosquitoes and leeches. It seems impossible, but still, I am curious; I decide that I will ask the Corpsman later, the "Doc" knows all about that sort of thing. Halfway across the grass-choked valley we cross a swift chest-deep stream; as I cross I try to wash away the red mud that covers me. The usual procedure would be to stop, set up security and fill our empty canteens, but the rain has provided us with more water than we need; we continue to move. The climb up the other side of the valley is harder yet. The rain is driving; it is difficult to hear above the noise as the huge drops pound the jungle canopy above us. Each time we take a break, we have to remove the leeches. The grenadier that is following me has a leech in his ear; a very serious problem will develop if it reaches the inner ear. The Corpsman comes up and removes it with insect repellant. He opens his Unit-1 medical kit and brings out a bottle of red-brown antiseptic that will clean and protect the bloody wound. When he opens the muddy kit, it is clean inside; it is as though he is opening a muddy oyster and as it opens, a beautiful, pure white pearl is suddenly exposed. All around the muddy green case, everything and everyone is caked with mud but the contents stored within the container remain sterile. I have noticed that anytime a Corpsman opens his Unit-1, Marines gather around to gaze into the bag with childlike amazement; everyone seems fascinated with the neatly packed contents.

We reach the peak of Hill 100 late in the afternoon. The rain is now a light drizzle; the hilltop is enveloped with fog. It is a dreary gray that surrounds us. The enemy could be only a few meters away; it is very eerie. We decide to remain here throughout the night. The rear point moves to place his Claymore along a likely avenue of approach; I watch as he disappears into the curtain of mist. He vanishes after walking a mere twenty feet down the slope; the curtain of fog closes behind him, leaving no trace. The grenadier and I move the other direction to set up the other Claymore. I stand watch as he screws the blasting cap into the top of the mine. The red-brown antiseptic on his ear is in sharp contrast to the black and green camouflage paint on his face. We return to the others; whispering loudly, we warn the team that we are coming in. The fog has covered the ground and is no more than waist high. I am barely able to locate my pack as we wade through the rolling gray soup. I look at the others and only their bush hats are visible above the layer of gray. Everyone is removing leeches and pulling cans of chow from their packs; I am hungry because I haven't eaten since the day before. I light a small piece of C-4 and heat a packet of instant coffee to which I have added four packets of sugar. The sweet, hot coffee tastes good and suddenly, I don't want anything else. I seldom have an appetite in the bush; often I either give my rations to my teammates or punch holes in the green cans and bury them. I have learned to carry as much food as the others, not because I may become suddenly ravenous, but because without the weight of the rations I will be expected to carry more of the team gear. As we finish eating, it grows darker and watches are assigned; exhausted from the day's hump, I wrap myself into the wet, muddy, plastic and drift into a deep sleep. The black of night passes and as the gray of dawn arrives … it is time to hump again.

We move toward Dong Ma Mountain. It is our third day and we hope to reach the objective sometime the following day. My feet have become numb but at times they feel raw; I decide that when we stop for the night I will take my boots off and check them, they have been wet for far too long now. The day's hump is a repeat of the day before and of the day before that. The rain has slowed to a constant drizzle that rattles on the brim of my bush hat. Mosquitoes are constantly on the attack, the steady hum and whine that they make only stops when they land to feed. Because of the endless rain, the insect repellant is wasted; it only washes off.

As we climb the mountain named About Cao, I have spotted a bunker. The TL comes up and dropping to one knee, we watch the dark entrance closely for movement. The rest of the team moves forward, forming a hasty perimeter. The TL and I go ahead to search the bunker. The entrance is a small slit formed from logs. Surrounding the bunker are numerous spider holes; the holes are just deep enough for an enemy soldier to stand and fire his weapon. Each has a roof made from logs and is covered with dirt and leaves. There are cobwebs in the entrances; the bunker and spider holes have not been used in some time. With the rest of the team, we search the area and locate a vast complex of bunkers and trenches. The enemy grunts are very disciplined; they have left nothing behind. We advise the people in the rear of our find. This was a large unit that bivouacked here, perhaps a reinforced company … perhaps larger. Satisfied that the bunker complex is abandoned, the TL points toward Dong Ma Mountain and we continue to move; there is no end to the muddy terrain. Occasionally I look back at the rest of the team and though they are a ragged, pitiful sight, each man is maintaining the proper interval and every eye scans the thick jungle for the enemy. The mosquitoes that we kill are gorged with blood, perhaps the blood of the enemy. Where did they go? How can a unit that large move so freely without being seen?

At last we can see the summit of our objective, Dong Ma Mountain. She rises from the lower jungle and stands defiantly against the gray, black sky like the queen of bitches that she is; the

Entrance to a North Vietnamese bunker complex found by our team. Somewhere deep within the Annam Cordillera, fall 1967.

"bitch queen" is only dominated by her larger "bastard brother," Dong Ha Mountain. We will patrol between the brother and sister and await the team that will relieve us in four or five days.

To our north we see helicopter gun ships making strafing runs on the jungle. Brilliant flashes come from them as rockets leave

Opposite: Moving toward the triple canopy of Dong Ma Mountain, September 1967. Typical of the terrain in Northern I Corps area. Due to the steep mountains, our movement was often restricted to less than 100 meters per hour.

their tubes. Streams of orange machine gun tracers disappear into the thick jungle. The Force Recon team has made contact with the enemy less than three kilometers from our present position. The secondary radio operator switches to their frequency. In the quiet of the jungle, the sounds of Marine and North Vietnamese gunfire can be heard coming from the handset of our PRC-25 radio. They are in heavy contact and have called for an extraction. We continue to move toward our objective; the thought of our brothers fighting for their lives has quickened our pace. I wonder if that team has met the enemy that lived in the bunker complex. I worry about the Battalion Recon team we passed to our southeast; they need to be advised of the enemy presence. The radio operator whispers each new development as though he is the announcer at a baseball game. Then the inevitable comes from the announcer ..."They are calling for blood, and plenty of it." The med-evac number of the wounded Marine is given; it is the TL. His blood type is given again; frantically, the team begs for the blood. The wounded man is just beginning a six month extension of his tour; he is an old friend. Silently, I wish him well. Now we can see the brilliant white-green and white-purple enemy tracers coming up from the black jungle seeking the gun ships; still firing, the sleek choppers begin evasive maneuvers. In the dismal overcast and sheets of rain, the enhanced enemy tracers resemble large burning balloons that are floating from the earth. There is nothing that we can do to help our friends; though frustrated, we must keep moving. Now I forget the pounding rain. My ever-present companion, "Fear," has once again joined me; his presence heightens my awareness and gives me strength. Our enemy is very near; aided by my companion, my vision penetrates deeper into the impenetrable walls of thick bamboo, scanning, seeking ... searching for the inevitable ambush.

Dark approaches and we search for a place to harbor for the night. We have reached the summit of Dong Kio; tomorrow we will reach our objective. The TL points toward a thick stand of bamboo and we move into it; as we settle into a perimeter, the radio operator announces that the embattled team has been extracted and there is no more word. He switches back to the artillery frequency and the TL plots the on-call concentrations. I remove one of my boots and am not prepared for what I see; the foot is a wrinkled mass of putrid milk-white flesh and is badly cracked and bleeding. With the ragged boot in one hand and my weapon in the other, I crawl through the matted bamboo to the Corpsman; after a quick glance he tells me that there is nothing that he can do, his feet are in the same condition. It is immersion foot; trench foot was what our grandfathers called it in France. One by one each of my teammates removes one boot at a time and stares in repulsion at the condition of their feet. Whispered curses are hurled toward Dong Ha and to those that sent us on this long march. I try to dry the foot but I have nothing that is not waterlogged. Finally, in desperation, I place the wet socks under the shoulder holster; perhaps my body heat will dry them. There is nothing more that I can do so I pull the muddy jungle boot back on, lace it up, and try to forget about my ravaged feet. Sleep is fleeting throughout the cold, wet night.

Dawn comes and we must reach the summit of Dong Ma today. We are suffering from exposure and the constant rain has chilled us to our bones. Now the cough medicine does little to warm us, but it feels good going down, like molten lead. We wolf down cold rations, never looking at the labels on the cans. The TL comes over to me; the wet cigarette in his mouth shakes violently as he shivers. He has taken the 7 × 50 field glasses from his pack and scans the two kilometers of steep jungle that we must climb, searching for signs of enemy activity. As he searches, I hold my bush hat over the glasses like an umbrella. The effort is wasted; the rain has fogged the glass, there is nothing to clean the tinted lenses with, everything is either wet or caked with mud. We don't have to speak with words; he merely gives me a look and I begin the day's hump.

We are moving from the harbor site when I see the enemy soldier. I freeze; he has not seen me. The TL comes up cautiously and without speaking I point at the lone man. The enemy grunt is standing in a small clearing; he is wearing a sheet of clear plastic fastened at the neck. Under the clear plastic he is wearing a long sleeved green shirt. I can see that he is armed with an AK. We move closer, now I can see that he is wearing a pair of baggy green trousers that are rolled up to the knees. Across his chest, packed into an ammo vest, are a few thirty-round AK magazines and a number of Chi Com grenades. Around his neck is a navy blue and gray-checkered scarf. His black hair is matted from the rain. I aim my rifle at the unsuspecting enemy soldier and wait for the order to fire; it does not come. If we kill him and he has friends nearby, a serious firefight is predictable. We may not be able to evacuate anyone that is wounded and it is doubtful that we will be extracted in this weather; we have learned this lesson at the expense of the team that was to our north. The soldier is standing between our objective and our position; he is searching the hills from where we have come. I wonder if we were spotted earlier. If so, there will be a prepared ambush nearby. The TL decides to detour and it is a good decision. The radio operator is told to report the sighting as soon as possible; we begin to move away from the enemy sentry. Our mission is to reach and patrol the saddle between the two mountains and then establish a landing zone for the relieving team; that is our priority. We will move on to our area of responsibility and once safe on the high saddle we can call artillery from nearby Camp Carroll if we wish.

We have moved to the south of the lone soldier; there is no doubt that there is a sizable enemy unit hidden nearby. I leave the team and move forward alone to scout our route. We have been trained to work ourselves out of these situations. After moving thirty or forty meters, I search the area thoroughly before signaling the team forward. Reaching my position, they move into a hasty perimeter and once again I move forward to scout the next few meters. We will continue this method of movement until the TL is satisfied that we are safe from ambush. Having moved around the enemy soldier, we advise the radio relay of the sighting. By early afternoon, we have reached the summit of Dong Ma Mountain. To the south, I am able to clearly see Camp Carroll, our artillery support base. It is a comforting sight and suddenly I do not feel so alone. The TL does not want to stop here; we are still too close to the enemy sentry. He decides to move onto the saddle and find a defendable harbor site before dark. There is an area of short elephant grass that must be crossed to reach the safety of the jungle. We move down the mountain a short distance so that we are not silhouetted on the ridgeline. We are moving with extreme caution; the selector on my M-16 is switched from "Safe" to "Auto"; I am concerned with the reliability of the brand new weapon. Having only test fired the four magazines, I do not fully trust the rifle yet. The rain has suddenly returned in driving sheets and I can barely see thirty meters ahead.

Dark is approaching fast and the wind-driven rain has blocked out most of the remaining light. We have reached a large, flooded bomb crater that will be our refuge for the night. Before we move into the muddy depression, the TL changes his mind and we move on for a few additional meters into a thicket of bamboo. We will sleep here and if the enemy comes we will use the nearby crater to fight from. The rain is now a deluge and the radio operators are having problems sending and receiving. This would be the very worst time to be attacked; visibility is minimal, our communication is faulty and evacuating any wounded by helicopter is probably impossible. The TL wants to move again, we must find a place that can be defended. If we are being watched, we will be attacked after dark; the enemy knows that they are safe from jets and gun ships in this weather, we cannot allow them to locate our night position. We move to another location and force our way into a much thicker stand of bamboo. We all agree that it offers little protection from an assault. It is growing darker and the TL tells me to move out of the bamboo and locate a place that we can defend for a lengthy firefight. When it becomes completely dark he will bring the rest of the team. It is a smart move, but we will have trouble plotting our artillery on-calls in the dark. He follows me to the opening that we have just entered through and tells me to be careful. I slip into the dusk and begin to crawl toward an area of trees that were blown down by an old air strike. As I crawl, I am almost swimming through the wet elephant grass. When I reach the first of the huge downed trees, I slide over the thick, splintered log and into a flooded bomb crater; unable to stop sliding down the slick slope of the crater, I enter the stagnant red water headfirst. Though I have managed to hold the new rifle up and it is spared the baptism, everything else is soaked with the red slime.

I climb back up to the log and continue my search for the

harbor site; it is dark and the others will be coming, I must hurry. I find a pile of thick logs that should stop AK rounds and perhaps offer protection from RPG rockets. Through a narrow opening I squirm between the muddy splinters and find myself inside a natural bunker. There is a sharp searing pain deep in my knee, it burns like venom; have I entered the den of a cobra? I cannot see in the dark pile of splintered logs and I know that this would be an excellent place to encounter Ho Mang. Flailing wildly with the rifle butt, I push myself into a corner of the log pile. I frantically kick into the dark, imagining myself trapped alone in the cobra den. After removing my muddy leather bush glove, I feel the wound and I am relieved to find that rather than snake bite, a very large splinter has embedded itself into my knee. I am not able to see the wound but I feel the long, thick piece of wood sticking through my trouser leg; the cloth is pinned to the flesh. The barbed splinter is difficult to remove but with a few repeated tugs it comes free.

The team is already moving toward me, I can hear the faint sound of elephant grass being parted. I aim my rifle toward the sound in case it is the enemy in the black void; totally alone in the dark, my mind races. The TL searches for me with strained whispers; recognizing his voice, I answer. When the team reaches the small muddy opening they slide through one man at a time. I hear the ripping of material as jackets and trousers snag on the sharp splinters. Whispered curses mingle with the deafening rain and sucking sounds come from boots being freed from deep, soft mud. Prodding whispers come from outside the tiny fortress as the TL hurries the team through the splintered fangs, the soft, cold, mud is miserable but the logs should stop rifle fire. The TL crawls toward me and tells me that he wants everyone awake; I tell him not to worry because in this driving rain there will be no sleep. I only want to get through this terrible night, tomorrow will take care of itself; the long night passes slowly and as I predicted, sleep evades the muddy sty. The knee burns and throbs; I can almost feel the infection setting in from the septic mud. I consider telling the Corpsman but I know that there is little that he can do in the dark. I try to keep it bleeding, and finally take the battle dressing from its place in my right cargo pocket and tie it around the wound.

It is a cold, filthy and painful night and I wonder if it will ever end. I can see illumination rounds drifting above Camp Carroll and as they float to earth under white parachutes, they seem ghost-like in the rain and dark. Their eerie glow throws small shards of dim light into our muddy fortress. We stare through the spaces in the logs, out into the rain, waiting for the enemy to come. At times we hear things but it is probably just the driving rain or scavenging rats. I wonder if the sentry has moved into a dry tunnel or bunker; it is an endless, miserable night that is stubbornly reluctant to leave.

Before dawn and without eating, we leave the log pile and move up the steep ridgeline toward Dong Ha Mountain. We are covered with mud from the long night among the logs. Our primary radio is not working and as we move the radio operator has dismantled the handset and searches frantically for the problem. Switching frequencies, the secondary radio operator has asked the relay when we will be relieved. The answer is what we expected; it will not be today. We move toward the thick-canopied jungle that covers Dong Ha Mountain. The TL will find a place to set up an observation post and we will stop moving for a while. We are weak from the exposure and we have had little or no sleep in days. The rain continues; mud from my baptism in the crater is washed into my pack and magazine pouches. My clothes are stained red from the stinking ooze; it has transformed itself from mud into some type of living entity. This is our sixth day. I have reached the point where I don't care anymore; I am just putting one foot in front of the other.

We find a good place to observe the valleys below. The Claymores are out and we will take turns resting. I open a can of peanut butter and some chocolate candy and wolf it down. Searching in my pack for other sources of sugar, I decide on a packet of powdered cocoa and a tin of pineapple jam. I don't bother to mix the powder with water and heat it, I just pour it from the paper package directly into my mouth and then take a drink from a canteen; I shake my head violently to mix the ingredients. The cocoa and stagnant bomb crater water mixes in my mouth and turns into chocolate syrup. Then the jam is mixed with the chocolate and the combination is unbelievable. The TL passes me the cough medicine and I take a deep drink. I am beginning to feel the warmth from the sugar and the medicine, so I take another drink before passing it on to the outstretched hand of the grenadier. With a huge grin that cracks the mud on his face, he announces in a whisper that he will take two drinks as well. When I decide to put the socks back on, there is only one left. I must have lost the other in the log-pile. Though disappointed beyond words, I reason with myself that it is for the best. Sitting against a splintered log, I try to smoke a cigarette in the rain, the TL tells me to get some sleep, and with the rain falling on my face I drift into unconsciousness. When I wake, it has stopped raining but the overcast is much darker; the jungle now has a rich, musty smell that reminds me of earthworms. The TL has his codebook out and has once again asked for an extraction time. It will go tomorrow if the weather allows it. It is beginning to rain again so we are sure that we will be here for a few more days. The Corpsman is concerned about our feet. We have traversed fourteen kilometers of rough terrain, but in reality we have probably traveled at least twenty-five kilometers due to the deep ravines and steep slopes of the mountains. We are where we are supposed to be and now it is time to be relieved. I look far below to the savage river that flows from west to east along Route 9. I scan the jungle-lined banks until I am sure that I see the place where we lost the Sergeant. It was only a few days past, but now it seems like many long months ago. I wonder if it was worth his life, just to reach the peak of this obscure mountain that smells like earthworms. I tell myself not to think about it … "it don't mean nothing."

Dark approaches and we move to another location for the night. We hope that our extraction will come early. My knee is swelling; it has become infected from the embedded splinter. The search for a place to set in takes us up the slope of Dong Ha Mountain or Nui Dong Ha to be exact, which translates into "the mountain of the river grotto." We move into a thick stand of bamboo that has huge boulders strewn through it; there is canopy above that deflects much of the rain. As the dark arrives, we are still without our primary radio. Both of the radio operators have crawled under a poncho to use a flashlight in an attempt to find and solve the problem. From under the muddy poncho drifts the electronic jargon that is of no interest to the rest of the team. The TL waits impatiently outside the poncho, and as the radiomen report their progress in the alien electronic language, the TL loses his patience and asks in a loud whisper, "Is that piece of crap ever gonna work?" The TL orders the secondary operator out from their muddy shelter and tells him to send a message to the relay advising them of our radio situation. If we lose the secondary radio during the night, we will be in serious trouble. Since there is nothing I can do to help, I fall asleep. I am prodded awake at midnight. The TL is calling a fire mission from Camp Carroll; we have movement nearby. The rain is pounding the canopy above and in the deafening noise no one bothers to whisper. I crawl over to the radio and listen as the fire mission is sent to the waiting artillery battery. The frequency is changed constantly as messages are sent to the relay and the fire mission is called. The TL hurls curses toward the manufacturers of the PRC-25 field radio. The ability to receive on the remaining radio is becoming broken. My knee is burning like fire and swelling with infection. The first 155mm round screams into the jungle below us. An adjustment is given and the second round arrives splitting the distance between the first round and our position. The team leader orders "fire for effect" and a volley of 105mm and 155mm rounds tear into the mountain, uprooting ancient trees and churning the muddy jungle floor. The rain muffles the artillery blasts and makes it difficult to determine distances. The mission is completed. When morning arrives we will move down to the impact area and check for enemy casualties. It is another dismal rain-swept night.

At first light we are moving down the mountain toward the blasted area. The rain has not stopped during the night and it continues to pound the jungle. We approach the area that was ripped and shredded from the howitzers. Although the rain is still driving, smoke boils from the ground. The heavy smell of detonated high explosives and burned bamboo engulfs the mountain. We continue through the devastated area, working our way back down the steep mountain. Below I see the logs that we harbored in; I signal the team to take cover. The TL intends to set in and observe the ridgeline that runs back to where the sentry was spotted. The team moves into a perimeter and we search the ridgeline for movement. A message is sent to the relay that our rations are almost gone but our major concern is that the remaining radio is faulty. I dump all of the cans of food from my pack and pass it around. I want to shed the weight; like a selfish child I have kept my hoard of sugar, coffee, cocoa and peanut butter. The coded reply arrives; such a quick response can only mean bad news, we already know the answer before being told. The ATL translates the coded message into "extraction date uncertain." We continue to observe the ridgeline and pray that we do not have to fight in this weather with faulty communication equipment.

The rain pounds us all day and as dusk approaches we move toward a place to harbor for the night. My knee is swollen and burns fiercely; I decide to show the Corpsman when we stop moving. We find a hidden place in high elephant grass that offers another excellent vantage point for observing the ridgeline. The TL places artillery concentrations along the ridge and up the mountain behind us; we must assume that our communication will continue to deteriorate. Artillery concentrations are plotted until there will be no need to adjust the fire; with so many plots the TL can order all on-calls fired and blow the entire ridgeline away. I crawl over to the Corpsman and show him the swollen knee. The "Doc" wants to open and drain the abscess while there is still daylight. He cuts a one-foot opening into the leg of the trousers with a shiny pair of scissors, exposing a shiny purple and red lump on the inflamed knee. From his kit, a hypodermic syringe emerges; I have seen this procedure before and I plead with him to just apply medicine to it. Everyone wants to watch and they find humor in my torment as the thick needle slides through the purple skin, deep into the infection. The pain takes the breath from my lungs; I watch the syringe fill with a yellow-white fluid. He pulls back harder on the plunger and blood shoots into the glass tube. When it is filled, he removes the needle and squirts the disgusting fluid into the brush, then he plunges the needle deeper into the swollen knee. When he is satisfied that the knee is drained, he produces a fresh syringe and fills it with antibiotic cream. I almost cry out as the new needle goes in and the white medicine shoots from the syringe into the wound. A quick gauze bandage is applied and he moves on to check the rear point's bleeding feet. I stare at the clean, white bandage and realize that it will soon be caked with mud. The TL passes the cough medicine and as I take two drinks, I lash out, telling him that I quit. *"I quit the Marines, I quit the war and I refuse to stay out here for another night, they have gotten their last kilometer out of me."*

He and the others with hands to their mouths are laughing hard, the ATL is choking as he tries to muffle the noise with his bush hat. My friend the TL asks, why do I want to quit when we are having so much fun? He reminds me that we are on a treacherous mountain in a driving storm, possibly a typhoon, we are cut off from Rt. 9 by the raging river below, we have no food, no radio, the enemy is very near and my leg will probably develop gangrene before too long. Through laughter, the team is enjoying a much-needed release of frustration and anxiety; burying my face into my poncho to muffle the sound, I join them. The laughter comes from deep within and adds to the shivering; I am shaking violently as repressed frustration leaves with the laughter. Each man adds fuel to the continued release; I feel lighter having emptied myself of the bottled-up emotions. Now, the entire team has quit the war, and the TL tells the radio operator to send the message to Dong Ha informing them that the entire team has quit. The TL is suddenly reminded that the radios are not working. This is more than we can take, gasps for breath mix with the uncontrolled choking laughter that engulfs the harbor site; like my teammates, I bury my face even deeper into my muddy poncho to muffle the waves of laughter that flow from my guts. Tomorrow is our eighth day in the pounding rain.

My body still aches from the emotional release as I roll into my wet poncho and drift into deep sleep. The night passes slowly and at dawn we hear the sound of helicopter engines in the distance. Everyone searches the gray sky in the direction of our base at Dong Ha. The radio operator is beside himself as he lets us know that it is our relief. The TL orders the Claymores blown; they will take care of any enemy lurking in the area. As the "hellboxes" are hammered, the rain is briefly blown away from us but quickly returns. We gather our gear and move onto the ridgeline. The radio operator directs the lead chopper to our position. We are being extracted by CH-34s; they will only pick up four of our team at a time. We move into a very wide perimeter to provide security for the extraction. The lead pilot wants to know about enemy activity and after being given the position of the enemy sentry, the escort gun-ships are dispatched to provide covering fire if needed. The lead ship calls for a yellow smoke. Behind me I hear the spoon release from a smoke grenade; with a prolonged hiss, the canister spews a bright yellow fog across the ridgeline. The lumbering old reliable chopper approaches and the rotor wash blows the thick yellow smoke into our eyes and throats. We see the first four of the heavily laden relief team jumping out. Four of our team climb aboard and the old chopper climbs from the mountain and disappears into the heavy overcast. As we wait for the second lift, the newly arrived team is telling us about the contact that we saw to the north of us. The team was mortared and the TL bled to death on the way to Delta-Med; it is a blow to us.

Immediately, the other chopper approaches and we run toward it. The second four men of the relief team jump off and we climb aboard; I do not recognize one of the men, perhaps he is a replacement that has arrived recently. In passing, our eyes meet and from my hideous appearance he must know that he is in for a terrible time; because of the deafening engine noise, I can only mouth the words "good luck." The relief team will have to move fast and hard because the enemy that lurks so close has seen the helicopter activity; now he will either lob mortars or send a unit to investigate. In the brief seconds that it takes the helicopter to lift from the LZ, the fresh team has disappeared into the safety of the thick jungle; in the privacy of my mind I pray that they stay safe. As we gain altitude, I watch the black, green mountain disappear below into the gray mist. Safe inside the vibrating helicopter, I suddenly realize that this is the first time in many days that we have been out of the rain.

11

The Chi Com

I was born alone
I will die alone
And between these two
I am alone day and night....
                    —Sengai

We have been inserted, by helicopter, three kilometers north of Nui Cay Tre. To the Vietnamese, Nui Cay Tre means "the mountain of bamboo"; to the grunt it is known as Mutters Ridge. The name came from the radio call sign of the Third Battalion, Fourth Marine Regiment who assaulted and dislodged the North Vietnamese 324 B Division during Operation Prairie the year before.

This is our fourth day of climbing through these mountains. Though it has been raining for well over a week, we were inserted during a break in the weather. We were sent here to assess the damage done by a recent B-52 attack. The hundreds of flooded bomb craters have turned the once lush rainforest into a sea of red mud. In the foul stench of the valley below, we found the scattered remains of our enemy. We can only report that there are an undetermined number of dead North Vietnamese in the valley. The bodies and pieces of bodies are mixed with the red mud, making it impossible to determine which is which. We have followed a shallow

A CH-46 troopship travels north. Crossing the Cam Lo River, the helicopter carries a Recon team towards Mutter Ridge.

stream through the carnage; on the map it is called Khe Khi, "the stream of monkeys." The Khe Khi flows into another shallow stream that runs north through the floor of the valley, on our map it is called Tre Nai, which in Vietnamese means "bamboo deer." We do not understand the meaning; it must be an ancient name that has been corrupted through the centuries. After meandering for an additional four kilometers, it empties into the Ben Hai River. The burned and blasted jungle has been transformed into the background of a nightmare; very few of the once towering hardwood trees have escaped the devastation brought by carpet-bombing. The leeches have survived and are all over us; they attack from the wounded trees and the plowed ground.

We are moving to reach the high ground on the north side of the valley before dark. Our exhausted team is venturing into the

DMZ and as we climb we realize that there is nothing in front of us but the hostile homeland of an unforgiving, merciless foe. We have not been able to maintain steady radio contact with the relay for days because the mountains intermittently block transmissions; we hope to establish better radio contact before dark. I want the rain to continue because when it stops, the mosquitoes arrive in swarms; from my position at point, I am convinced that the leeches are concentrating on me. The mountain that we are moving up is steep and as we climb we hold onto tree trunks that have been splintered by the onslaught of bombs. We move from tree to tree; without them the mud would make the climb impossible. To the south, across the wide valley, a cloud-enveloped Nui Cay Tre looms ominously above us. Until we reach the peak, we are vulnerable to the watching eyes of enemy forward observers. Occasionally, I glance below deep into the shadowed floor of the devastated valley and think of the horror that we encountered there.

As if the B-52 attack did not rain enough hell, the mountain that we are now climbing has been attacked by countless sorties of Phantom jets delivering "snake and nape." The splintered, tortured tree trunks are black and charred from the napalm and the oily gel that did not ignite has mixed with the red mud, turning it into a texture similar to axle grease. My pack and ammo belt are waterlogged and have picked up extra weight from the greasy mud. I consider dumping my remaining water and chow, but I will need it later. The mud has clogged the lug soles of our jungle boots and it is difficult not to slip; we know that if we lose our footing we will end up at the bottom of the mountain. I use my weapon to climb, digging the stock into the mud as a brace while I grab the next bomb-blasted tree trunk. The oily napalm has lubricated the entire mountain, it has soaked into the burned trees; we have to grasp each splintered trunk in a hug. The black M-16 no longer resembles a rifle; it is encased within a shapeless red blob of sticky mud. After awhile, I have to use my Ka-Bar to climb with. I stab the earth ahead and then pull myself up; the deep, soft mud soon renders this effort useless. The team is strung out down the mountain; I can hear the gasps for breath coming from them. They no longer look like Marines; the axle-grease mud has absorbed them into the mountain, only by the human-like shapes are they recognized from the rest of the red, oily sea. I keep glancing to the south, across the valley, toward the towering black of Mutters Ridge that stands a few kilometers away. The gray-black clouds are churning around her; long thin fingers of the gray mist seem to force their way through the thick canopy and emerge hundreds of meters away only to once again repeat the pattern as if weaving. I continue to worry about the enemy mortars that are certain to be dug in deep along the slopes of the mountains and in the deep ravines along the valley floor. Waves of panic mix with frustration as the mud becomes more difficult, slowing the climb and forcing us to linger under the eyes of the enemy gunners like tempting bait. I begin to climb faster, fighting the mud, using all of the strength that has been kept in reserve.

I have reached the top and I fall out. Exhausted, I drag my tired body behind a blasted log and try to catch my breath. I am too tired to care about the hungry leeches; ignoring them, I allow their feast to continue unmolested. I look around at the rest of the team as they reach the top. Each is covered with oily mud and is loudly sucking air; their eyes are red from the napalm fumes and tears stream down their mud caked faces. I want to reach out and help them climb the last few agonizing meters, but I have nothing left to give. Instead I just nod my head to each as they struggle past. As I lay in the cold mud I am enjoying the softness of it; there has never been a bed so comfortable. I take out a canteen and pour it over my mud-caked rifle; scraping the mud from the receiver, I eject the round from the chamber and replace the magazine with a fresh one. After moving through the foul stench of the valley and the fumes of the napalm, the clean air here on the summit is an elixir I can feel my lungs absorb the oxygen.

The team leader wants to move on. He is unable to give the order without pausing for long, deep, struggled breaths. Gasping, he can only nod and point the direction we will move. We are now on a long ridgeline, there is no arguing, we are exposed and per-haps a forward observer is calling for mortars this very moment. Using the rifle as a brace, I force myself onto my feet and begin to move. My knees buckle under the burden of my pack; rain and mud have increased its weight. As we move along the flat ridge, I feel as though I could start running yet I cannot feel my wobbling legs or feet; the hard climb has left my legs numb. It is only by the sucking sounds that my boots make in the mud that I am able tell that I am actually walking. Radio contact has once again been established and our position is sent to the impatient radio relay; they have been concerned by our failure to report each hour. The radio operator is gasping for breath as he sends the coded coordinates. I can hear his voice struggling as he sucks in the clean air. We will search for a safe place to rest and send the hard earned information of the carnage in the valley to the intelligence people that we curse each day; perhaps they will believe us, perhaps they won't, to us it no longer matters. I filled six canteens from a bomb crater earlier and I only drank one as we climbed the mountain. I plan use them to clean the mud off of my face and rifle later. There are more flooded craters; there will be plenty of water. The rain does not clean mud, it will clean everything else but it has a pact with mud. They are allies with the heat and the jungle. Each only wants to torture and make me miserable.

Our exhausted column is moving along the ridge when I spot a small pile of metallic debris ahead. Closer inspection reveals that it is part of an aircraft of some type, perhaps a helicopter. Whatever it is, it was stripped long ago and has been abandoned. The team leader is trying to make out the faded numbers from what appears to be the fuselage; he copies them in his notebook. Satisfied that it is probably a known crash, we move on. Some of the team has begun to complain that the unexploded napalm is burning their skin; our eyes are still streaked with tears.

The ridge soon becomes choked with dense, short elephant grass, perhaps six feet in height; after the stench in the valley, the grass is very fragrant. Soaked with red oily mud, we are in sharp contrast to the clean green grass. Encased in the greasy mass, it is difficult to determine our equipment from our clothing; we have been transformed into slithering indefinable shapes. If we locate a crater that is deep enough, I will try to swim around in it, maybe the mud will come off. I hope that we will stop and set up an observation post soon because the view is great from up here on the ridge. Three kilometers below is the Ben Hai River and from this vantage point we can see deep into North Vietnam and toward the batteries of hostile artillery. As I break out of the elephant grass, I hear movement to my right and to my front. Suddenly from nowhere, there is a Chi Com grenade just ahead of me in the mud; smoke is coming from the hollow wooden handle. The grenade looks new; the picture remains frozen in my mind. There is no time to consider options—I am only able to react. With my right hand I pull the trigger on my rifle and throw my left arm over my face; as the empty brass flies in a continuous bright flashing stream from the mud-caked rifle, I hear bells ringing. I think that I dream of the grenade in the mud, maybe not. The dreams are wild, unorganized, they make no sense. I think I see people and places but I am not sure; I am not sure of anything. My mind is filled with a whirling kaleidoscope of blinding colors disrupted with surreal visions. I hear voices; they are calling me. Nausea follows me through the dark of an echo-filled hall; each vision is shattered by the next as if they are glass panes, yet the sounds are not of breaking glass but are of moans and cries and perhaps deep, hideous laughter.

When I wake it is for a brief moment; I see only the black and gray streaked sky. I cannot hear anything. The ringing is in my mind not in my ears. I am on my back, my arms are beside me and I can feel the cold mud under my head. My jungle jacket is smoking; I think that someone has dropped a cigarette on me; nothing makes any sense. I roll my head to the left and lying beside me is a North Vietnamese soldier. His face is only inches from mine and he is looking at me with his eyes open. He is wearing a faded green shirt; the top button is buttoned. His thick black hair is enhanced due to the contrast against his paste white skin. His eyes are blank but one continues to blink rapidly. Blood begins to appear in thin streams from his nose and mouth; for the brief moment that we share, we become brothers. As I stare at him I think he dies; I look the other way and see my team members throw a green smoke grenade. I think that I hear the popping sound of a helicopter engine … I dream again.

I realize that I am awake. I am on a table and there is a brilliant light in my eyes. I am completely naked and someone above in the light mentions that they have never seen such a filthy bastard. Someone else is pulling tiny grenade fragments from my arms and legs with large tweezers. It must be a Navy doctor that is asking me questions. What is my name, where am I from, etc. I am not aware of the answers I give but since I was able to respond, my canvas stretcher is moved to a place on the floor out of the way. I look around and realize that I am inside Delta-Med, the hospital at Dong Ha. A Corpsman from our company has arrived and is telling me what has happened. I have a concussion from the grenade blast but all of the wounds are considered superficial. My ears were packed with the red mud and perhaps that is why I didn't hear anything. The grenade blast drove the mud into my ears, nose and mouth; it was the mud that absorbed the blast and saved me. I reach down and feel for my legs and genitals; the Corpsman assures me that they are intact. I look around the Triage and feel guilty. Wounded Marines and South Vietnamese soldiers on canvas stretchers litter the bloody concrete floor. My wound is nothing compared to what I see. I hear moans of pain and the noise of the med-evac helicopters just outside. The doctors and corpsmen have no time to bother with me, they have their hands full. The fatigued doctors order the blood-splattered stretcher-bearers to bring in the severely wounded first. One is looking at me as he barks the orders and I am sure that he is disgusted that I was brought here for a minor grenade wound. The Corpsman helps me to my feet and two wounded Marines that are now bearers immediately grab the stretcher that is caked with my mud.

I want to flee. The Doctor has made me feel ashamed. My arms and legs are stiff from the punctures and there is a jagged hole through my left forearm. I show the Corpsman that has come to retrieve me, I am told that they have no time to bother with it; he will fix the arm at our sick bay. I know that the arm kept the fragment from hitting me in the face or the throat. Now the pain is arriving, I want out of this place. My muddy jungle utility uniform was cut off of me, rendering it useless. The Corpsman gives me a green wool blanket to wrap up in; I pull on my muddy, worn out jungle boots and cringe as the cold mud oozes between my bare toes. Outside, the Delta-Med LZ is busy, the result of heavy fighting somewhere. Dead and wounded Marines are being offloaded from CH-34 and CH-46 helicopters; streams of blood streak their green sides while crimson stained bandages are blown across the steel matted LZ. Exhausted pilots and gunners, having seen too much and rested too little, look at us with tired eyes as they immediately leave for another load.

Due to the massive amount of wounded and dead, Delta-Med has become more of a processing center than a hospital. The wounded go one direction and the dead go another. A doctor and a Corpsman are moving from one stretcher to the next; they determine who is serious, who can be saved, and who will die. The terminally wounded are put aside; the Navy Chaplain is moving from one of these Marines to the next, giving last rites. He prays for each man regardless of faith and traces an invisible cross on foreheads that are covered with blood soaked bandages. The dead are taken across the LZ to the plywood shanty that houses the Graves Registration; next to it sits the gray International Harvester refrigerator truck that I fear; the mud-caked truck carries the filled bags to the airstrip where they are sent south to the Da Nang mortuary. The Corpsman leads me toward our jeep that sits alongside the truck, I want to retreat back into the dreams. I don't want to go near the gray truck or the plywood building. As we approach the back of the truck, the insulated double doors are open, revealing the stacks of bags; the truck is filled to capacity. Inside the building I see the naked feet of the dead, their stretchers in a straight line on the concrete floor. I pull the blanket up around my face and get into the jeep. Had it not been for my arm, would I also be going to Da Nang? The question will always be with me.

After the bouncing jeep ride, I am ushered into the plywood shack that is our sick bay. All of the Corpsmen gather around inspecting the many scrapes and punctures that the grenade left in me. One of the Corpsmen has a long wooden swab and after soaking the cotton tip in a bottle of a red antiseptic, he shoves it through the wound until the red tip emerges some three inches away. The pain is blinding; my knees buckle. Immediately, the antiseptic burns like a corrosive acid and I fight back the tears. To conceal the pain, I hurl curses and insults at my friends the Corpsmen. They seem pleased that the wound is "through and through." There are no pieces of grenade fragments in the wound. A bandage is applied; there will be no stitches because the wound must drain. Now another Corpsman moves behind me and after pushing aside the green wool blanket, he plunges a needle deep into my right buttock. As the thick antibiotic leaves the syringe, I bite my lip to endure the pain. Before the needle is withdrawn another Corpsman attacks with his needle and I am protected from tetanus. Two of my team members have arrived and have brought me a clean set of jungle utilities. I am given a handful of antibiotic pills and sent on my way. I ask the Corpsmen for some pain pills but there will be none. I am told to go get into my bunk and because of the concussion, not to drink any alcohol. One of them will check on me the following day. I thank the Corpsmen and then my teammates and I walk across the muddy road to the sanctuary of our hooch. More of my friends from other teams have arrived to hear about the grenade and the kill. My rifle and bush gear are on my canvas bunk. The team has cleaned the weapon for me ... it is immaculate. Yes, they are my family, and we are more than brothers, we are a hunting pack. Two bottles of Vietnamese whiskey are passed around. I am sure the Corpsmen know that drinking is the first thing I will do. When the bottle passes to me, I pour an inch of the gut-wrenching liquid into my canteen cup. Now, in the tin roofed lair, we will honor one another. In the dim, yellow hue of a naked light bulb, the pack will tell and then re-tell the story. Aided by the burning whiskey, the account will be repeated until each man has purged it from his mind and cleansed his soul. When the morning comes it will never be mentioned again.

I will receive a Purple Heart for this minor wound, my first of two. It is the same medal that will be given to the dead, is that fair? Should I refuse the award? I wonder about the dead NVA soldier. I ask my teammates. They are sure that he was the one that threw the grenade; our pack attacked and killed him immediately. The new man in our team shows me the dead man's rifle, a muddy AK with a metal folding stock; I am offered the prize but I refuse it. The new man can have it, there have been so many enemy weapons and there will be many more; soon he will also lose his interest in

119

souvenirs. The owner of the rifle was the only enemy soldier that we killed; after he was shot there was no more firing. The whiskey burns in my stomach as I tell them about watching him die; I want to share this with them, the burden is much too heavy to carry alone. I ask the new man to take one of the bottles of whiskey across the road to the Corpsmen. Still clutching his prize, he bounds out the door into the dark with the nearly full bottle. Having honored each other, we drink to the brave enemy grunt that was also our brother.

I want to go outside in the dark and wash but then I realize that they have cleaned me up in the Triage. They must have washed the mud off to find each tiny wound. The whiskey has taken all of the pain away but my hip throbs from the shot. Sleep is coming fast and now I will be allowed to rest. Quietly vanishing like the pack of wolves they are, the team moves next door to finish the bottle … the dreams return.

12

Notre Dame de La Vang

We have arrived at the Basilica of La Vang. Emerging from the dark of the Hai Lang Forest, some three kilometers to the south, we have come to this tranquil, holy place to rest and await the trucks that will return us to Dong Ha. It is a beautiful and serene setting filled with vibrant gardens and traversed by long, straight boulevards that are lined with colorful mimosa and fragrant frangipani; it seems to be more vision than reality. Those that inhabit this surreal wonder of beauty and stillness appear sheltered from the surrounding terror and carnage; not protected by razor wire and sandbagged bunkers, but rather by the invisible aura of faith. The grounds of the Basilica cover an area of at least one half of a grid square; the boulevards form the shape of the Holy Cross, at its axis sits a huge cathedral. Groups of nuns clad in black and white habit float through the gardens, while yet another is leading a group of small uniformed children that walk in double file holding hands, their embarrassed laughter punctuates a chorus of "Frère Jacques." Across the grassy expanse are the scattered statues of saints and of the Blessed Mother; this is truly a sanctuary in a sea of terror.

It was on these grounds that Catholics sought refuge in the deep rain forest as one hundred years of religious persecution swept the land. It was here during the first year of the persecution in 1798 that the Lady of La Vang first appeared to a small band of starving, fever ridden Christians that had fled from nearby Quang Tri.

The apparition of the Lady, which has reappeared numerous times, carries a small child in her arms with two angels at her sides. During this first apparition, the refugees were instructed by the Lady to make medicine by boiling the leaves from the *la'vang* tree; fevers were broken, lives spared, and La Vang would evermore be recognized as a place of healing.

Sitting adjacent to the site of the apparition, the gothic Notre Dame Cathedral has been placed on the very spot where thirty captive Catholics were burned alive in a single act of immolation. This was not the first church to be placed on this hallowed ground; completed in 1928, it is the third in a series that date to the first appearance of the Lady. Pilgrimages began immediately after the first apparition and continued through the years of persecution, although many were captured, tortured and martyred. With each pilgrimage came the tools that transformed the hostile jungle into this place of hope and tranquility. And even now, as air strikes sweep the surrounding mountains and jungle with rolling walls of fire and the ambush war continues ever so close; pilgrims stand their vigil, patiently waiting, patiently watching.

As we move through the fragrant gardens of this Holy place, I suddenly feel as though we are intruding; I feel impure. We are ragged and filthy with the blazing eyes that proclaim a successful hunt. Less than four kilometers from this peaceful refuge our pack hunted, bled, and then evaded the enemy ... so close to this sanctuary ... yet so far. Our four-man team, inserted into the Hai Lang Forest by helicopter, followed the Song Nhung upstream, toward its origin. As we continued southeast the little river became the slow moving crystal stream that twists and tunnels its way through the dark shadows of the deep rain forest; it was here that we found our enemy. Under the dark shade of triple canopy, where the clear narrow stream is lined with thick golden bamboo and where huge umbrella-like ferns create a dark corridor—it was here that our ambush was tested. In this ancient garden grotto of purple orchids where vine and rock have married, it was here that we killed as a pack. As we rested and filled our canteens, quietly hidden among the towering ferns and bamboo, three North Vietnamese soldiers suddenly emerged from the dark corridor. They moved directly toward us ... slowly wading through the knee-deep water. Dressed in dark green clothing, two of the three were armed, one with an SKS carbine, the other an AK. The third soldier, unarmed and wearing a green pith helmet, carried a large wicker basket. They carried the weapons slung across their backs as if unconcerned that their enemy may lurk nearby. There was no time for our team to flee into the shadows, the grenadier fired into the three soldiers with a flechette round that shredded everything in its path; joining the fury of the blast, our automatic rifles sent long bursts into the already dead soldiers. The stream filled with a carpet of floating debris ripped from the jungle by the hundreds of steel darts; the smell of freshly cut ferns and burned powder filled the corridor ... none of the three victims survived. With security provided by the grenadier, we moved through the bloody killing zone, collecting the two weapons and the basket. Never stopping to examine or search the obviously dead enemy, we continued across the narrow crimson stream and silently vanished into the dark of the canopy After moving a great distance from the ambush, we opened the basket only to find it full of small frogs ... many were ripped and torn from the onslaught of the flechette. We have met and destroyed a foraging detail; that explains the slung rifles. There is an enemy unit nearby. Our request for an extraction by helicopter is denied; trucks will meet us to the north. Fear arrives and forces his way in where he becomes allies with the shock that always accompanies a successful hunt. Now we will move north, leaving the Hai Lang and escaping the enemy that we must assume is in pursuit.

Exhausted from the days and sleepless nights of evading enemy patrols, here in the Basilica we have found an area of shade under an ancient Banyan tree; we will rest here while waiting for the trucks. We have been spotted by the singing children, the Nun allows them to approach our ragged little band; quickly, we try to straighten our hair and button our torn bush jackets in order to look presentable ... it is hopeless. Our jungle clothing is caked with six days of sweat and dirt, and as the sweat dried it left patches of crusty white residue on the faded green material.

The Nun is French, perhaps approaching middle age; she tells us that the children are from the school in Quang Tri. She knows the geography of North America and asks each of our team which locale we are from. She has seen my name that is stenciled across the back of my jacket along with my blood type. She asks *"Êtes-vous les français ... d'où êtes-vous?"* I explain to her that my father's family immigrated to America from Paris. *"Oui, votre nom est Francais."* Though her English is flawless, I make a clumsy attempt to speak *"en français."* My grammar is immediately corrected and the children laugh. She asks if they can join us in the shade, asthey are also waiting for transportation. We apologize for our appearance and explain that we have been in the mountains for at least a week. *"Oui ... c'est la guerre."* I worry that she has seen the extra rifles, their wooden stocks badly splintered from the flechette. The children gather around us, they sit very close, their innocent eyes searching ours. They look past the blazing embers of the predator until they find the last displaced thread of youth that has been suppressed back into the recesses of our souls, and like all children they are able to charm it forth and bring lost smiles to faces that have seen too much. And now ... tiny hands suddenly find their way into our hands, into the hands that have murdered the bearer of frogs. As the Nun and the children correct my grammar, I have briefly escaped the icy grip of fear and basked in this unusual pause from the ambush war.

Now we are joined by the ravaged, the homeless ... the scab is ripped loose to reveal those that have felt the fire of napalm and the deep torment of losing everything and everyone. They wait here, seeking help from the Lady; Mahayana prayer beads are entwined with the Rosary. We are offered slices of mango and pineapple; our provisions exhausted, we have nothing to share. I am sure that the foraged fruit is all that these people have to eat. The kind Nun peels the fruit for those with no arms; I watch as the hands that have soothed the torment of the afflicted and have bandaged lepers work tirelessly ... she does not eat until everyone has their share. Silently, I wonder what she has seen, where she has been; I admire her courage and strength, I feel small and foolish in her presence. As she peels the fruit she continues my French lesson while maintaining order with the children; she knows each of the scarred and maimed, occasionally she tells their story. The kind hands pass a large piece of sugary pineapple to me ... *"donnez-la à l'enfant, sil vous plait"* ... I do as she asks and hand it to the children sitting behind me. The ravaged sit with us, quiet smiles mask their pain; I try to avert my eyes from their horrible wounds.

In the distance our trucks approach the holy ground. An officer, sensitive to the serenity of this place, halts the small convoy. He is obviously much more mature and understands these things. Reluctantly, we don our bush gear; we receive hugs from the children and from the ravaged, I do not want to leave this place and these people. As we begin to move away, the Nun reminds me to never forget my French heritage and once again she tells me, sternly, to study my grammar. From each of the children comes the sad words of farewell ... *chao, hen gap lai ... bonne chance ... au revoir ... Dieu vous bénissent* ... we must answer each of them, they tug at our trouser legs until we recognize and answer each. The maimed still do not speak, yet they speak volumes with their eyes and quiet manner. We move along the boulevard to the waiting trucks; I look back occasionally and wave. The trucks have parked at the very edge of the Basilica. I realize that when we cross the invisible border we will once again become the pack of predators. The time that we have spent with the innocent is priceless; after the carnage that we inflicted in the Hai Lang, it has been a soothing experience. Will our youth ever resurface again? I want to return here someday and perhaps bring food and blankets; perhaps one of the Corpsmen will come with me and bring medical supplies but I know that this will not happen ... *c'est la guerre.*

As we climb onto the trucks I try not to look toward the shade of the ancient Banyan tree; I think that I could very easily walk away from the madness and stay with them forever. I think of the maimed that have been ripped and savaged, they never once asked us for anything and never thought of themselves as they shared the last of their meager forage. With quiet smiles they have offered us all that they possess. As the truck lurches ahead, I look away from my brothers as tears well in my eyes and begin to flow ... my heart has been broken.

13

In the Shadow of Co Roc

Our team has been inserted some five kilometers due south of Hill 881 South. The abandoned Special Forces camp at Lang Vei, located less than three klicks to the southeast, is visible from our recon zone. Eight kilometers to the east, the airstrip at Khe Sanh is being dismantled; the base is to be abandoned. The long, fierce battle that bled the North Vietnamese so dearly throughout the past winter and spring has left the vast expanse of fertile earth between the Rao Quan River and the Laotian border an endless churned moonscape from the constant assaults by B-52 bombers. The deep, dark red craters are in sharp contrast to the lush blanket of bright green elephant grass and black-green rain forest that covers the hills. Never has a place felt such wrath from conventional airpower and never has the North Vietnamese Army been so ravaged. It is summer 1968 … my second summer.

The battle is said to have ended months before, yet pockets of enemy remain; some are trapped, others left behind to hold key positions and to guard supply caches for future offensives. Assault battalions seem to appear from nowhere to attack Marine positions and then vanish back into Laos. The enemy dead that are left hanging in the barbed wire of firebase perimeters are much younger than those encountered before the battle; the failed Tet offensive has drained their infantry divisions of older, seasoned fighters. Recon teams are being used extensively to search out hidden supply

126

The author, holding a Chi-Com grenade, poses with NVA equipment captured during a patrol along the Laotian border during the summer of 1968. The assault rifle is Chinese, Type-56; the steel helmet is Soviet. Mortar rounds as well as RPG rockets can be seen in the foreground.

caches as well as to locate and monitor the movement of enemy troops across the Khe Sanh plateau.

Five kilometers to the southwest of our recon zone is Co Roc. It is, to us, the most ominous place in the world. A sheer black stone wall that rises abruptly 837 meters from the floor of Laos, Co Roc is the impregnable guardian fortress that overlooks the narrow D'Ai Lao pass at Lao Bao. Ancient vines have grown deep into the rock, concealing the huge caves that honeycomb the massif. It was from these caves that our enemy sent as many as 1, 300 rounds of artillery and rocket fire each day into Marine positions fifteen kilometers to the east. With a range of twenty-seven kilometers, the Soviet 130mm artillery pieces were able to strike every Marine position on the Khe Sanh plateau as well as the hill outposts with little effort.

The high grassy plateaus of Laos drift gently from the western slope of the Co Roc plateau; elephant herds that once grazed freely

127

Near Khe Sanh, spring 1968.

in the sweet, tall grass have sought refuge farther to the west, escaping the constant noise of combat. A few kilometers to the south is the impenetrable rainforest of the Bolovens Plateau, it is an ancient battleground that has, through countless centuries, been soaked with the blood of Siamese, Lao, Chinese, Cham, Mongol, Khmer, Vietnamese, Japanese, French and now, perhaps, American.

The steep wall does not actually begin or end but is in reality the eastern edge of a massive flat plateau. The wall turns south within two kilometers of the old prison at Lao Bao and meanders along the southern bank of the Xe Pon River, becoming much steeper and creating a natural border between Vietnam and Laos for some twenty-five torturous miles. It was here in the shadow of Co Roc that, for one hundred years, Vietnamese emperors unleashed frustrated fury against their hated Catholic captives; burning, starving, beheading, and humiliation only served to attract an even greater number of those seeking the sanctity of canonization. With Indochina held in the grip of French colonialism throughout the following century, the miserable legacy of Lao Bao continued; those that defied the authority of the colonial government were subjected to agonizing torments that would have left ancient emperors speechless with envy. Political dissidents, chained to bandits, thieves, murderers, rapists and warlords, rotted alive in sweltering concrete cell blocks; Lao Bao, unlike other penal colonies, was not so much a labor camp as it was a killing place. The wretched souls that were sentenced to this nightmare were without hope, having been thrust deep into the bowels of the partially subterranean prison for no other reason but to die from malnutrition, infection, tropical disease and snakebite. For those no longer wanting to struggle through the next day, a merciful death by strangulation could be purchased from a fellow prisoner for a single ration of thin soup.

The vast grounds of the old prison, rivaling most botanical gardens in Asia, were kept in a state of perfection by *Indo-chine* guards that enjoyed the unlimited labor force constantly at their disposal. Opulent, strutting peacocks that were utilized as vigilant sentries wandered freely within the walls of the compound; no movement escaped their attention and no coaxing could prevent the alarm sent by their shrill, frightened screeches. In an ambiance filled with terror, despair and seclusion, Lao Bao was just as much a confinement for the oppressors as it was for the oppressed; for many, the total isolation became an unbearable test of psychological stamina. For the three or four French *delegue* posted at the prison to oversee the *Indo-chine* guard detachment, solace was commonly found in the embrace of the abundant poppy.

Standing alone in the shade of a corrugated tin roofed shed was the vain and selfish Madame Guillotine; spoiled and arrogant, she unleashed her fury against criminals as well as those that would dare attempt to lift the yoke of colonialism from Indochina. The Madame was kept in a state of pampered perfection by suitors that were often picked from the very worst of those sent to die slowly in the dungeons; in time they would also feel her intimate caress. Often the botanical splendor became a gathering place for those that were invited to watch the spectacle of terror. The Madame, wearing a fresh coat of "widow-black" paint, her blade honed to deadly brilliance by the loving hands of future victims … would fall repeatedly. Crimson rivers ran from the concrete gutters beneath her bosom, carrying away the rebellious blood of martyred patriots. Each brilliant flash from the Madame turned the Xe Pon red and as the shallow river flowed slowly and deliberately south, the crimson defiance of Indochina was absorbed into the towering rock that transformed Co Roc into a darker shade of black.

Our four-man team moves west along an entangled streambed. We move from one massive bomb crater to the next, occasionally finding an unexploded bomb, a few have not completely tunneled into the earth. Their green shapes that protrude menacingly from the red dirt add yet another facet of terror for us to deal with. Bright yellow lettering still remains on the olive colored paint. The bombs look new and though delivered from miles above, we are surprised at the lack of damage the impact has made to their steel casings. Leading our tiny column, I try to avoid the deep craters but it is impossible, they are too congested; the muddy holes sap our strength as we slide down into their depths, wade through the stagnant green rain water and then climb fifteen feet up the slope to the opposite rim. When I encounter an unexploded bomb, I half-turn my back to the embedded menace as I would to a cold wind or driving rain. Though I may pass within mere inches of the green steel, this ridiculous effort is my futile attempt to escape being vaporized should it suddenly detonate; behind me the TL finds humor in my absurd actions.

Our team has often patrolled other heavily bombed areas and we are accustomed to devastation, but none of us has seen anything this severe. Continuing west, we encounter the familiar smell of death; our enemy utilizes the deep craters to bury their dead. Though the crude graves are easily located, we no longer report enemy cemeteries. Weeks before, while patrolling to the north, a recon team found a massive burial plot and immediately reported the position. A platoon of Marines was dispatched from Khe Sanh to dig through the putrid mud in order to count the enemy bodies. While the bloated, decomposing bodies were dragged from the grave; the team soon realized their mistake as muffled curses were hurled at them from beneath gas masks. We now have an unspoken

Moving through thick elephant grass near Khe Sanh in the spring of 1968.

understanding with our infantry brothers that the graves are to be left unmolested and unreported.

To our west the sun begins to set behind the black wall of Co Roc; brilliant, sparkling, diamond points of light appear briefly through the wall as the sun finds and weaves its way through tiny tunnels in the ancient rock. We move into a shallow crater that will be our harbor site for the long, moonless night. In the distance the earth vanishes into the black shadow that is cast from the towering cliff; soon the Xe Pon disappears, taking with it Route 9. We watch as the shadow moves rapidly toward our position. Maintaining a steady flow that resembles spilled ink, it moves across the hills and deep jungle-choked ravines, reaching into the depths of the craters, until suddenly, only the black void of night remains. We have not plotted artillery concentrations around our position; our RZ is beyond the range of support. Each member of our team knows that he has only the other three to depend on, with two Claymore mines, three M-16 rifles, four Colt .45 A-1 pistols and one M-79 grenade

131

launcher ... nothing more. The night is long and though radio watches are assigned, sleep does not come. We wait for the dawn and, as always, our eyes strain painfully as they search deep into the dark that we are immersed in. Hourly situation reports are sent to the radio relay atop of Hill 950 some three kilometers north of the Khe Sanh airstrip. The "sit-reps" are not sent in the form of words—we dare not speak in the black void; when the relay asks us to acknowledge his call, there are just the two distinct pauses in the constant squelch as the handset is keyed twice. The two small audible clicks are all that connects us with the world, and all that assures the relay that we have not disappeared into the liquid black night. The familiar voice of the radio operator manning the relay is comforting. He shares the long night with each of the teams that are scattered throughout the black void; like a mother hen he maintains a vigilant watch over us and is quick to scold if a "sit-rep" is not answered immediately. He is all that we have in the darkness.

During the night, in the distance to our west, we hear the very distinct sound of a truck engine. The report is coded and sent to the relay immediately; the noise drifts away until only the silent dark remains. Before the first light breaks to the east over the Khe Sanh plateau, we have already forced down the cans of cold, grease-caked rations and are moving from the crater. We move westward through the dark that seems so reluctant to leave, searching for the source of the engine sounds ... praying that we do not find it.

We move silently through the tall, dew soaked elephant grass and jungle knowing that there may be a truck parked or supply cache hidden nearby. The TL wants me to move into the streambed below before the sun arrives; the thick jungle that chokes the stream will offer excellent concealment as we move. We continue to the west as the bright rays of morning turn the sky into a brilliant array of blue, orange, white, yellow and perhaps red. The black face of Co Roc becomes a shining ebony jewel as the blazing sun forces the black shadow back into the massive wall. Just as it flowed from its source to overwhelm the earth and send it into a black abyss, the flood of black ink is absorbed back into the massif, where it will wait with the blood of martyrs, waiting impatiently to be summoned once more ... to devour the light and again bring the dark void.

The sun filters into the streambed through vines and ferns, bringing with it the steaming heat while casting shadows that blend with the trapped remnants of the night. Behind I hear the whispered voice of the TL as he gives our coded position to the radio operator to send to the relay. Our team is forced from the streambed as it changes direction and disappears into a wall of jungle to the south; in order to continue westward, we have no choice but to leave the safe haven and climb the wet, grassy slope to the ridge above. The ridge is covered with scattered stands of tall bamboo and thick, overgrown groves of banana trees. The banana trees have grown very close to one another; at times they create a wall that is almost too dense to move through. Their spongy, bright green stalks squeak loudly and cover us with sticky sap as we squeeze between them; the pungent, sweet smell is heavy in the fresh morning air. Thick nets of dew-drenched spider webs fill the empty spaces between the green stalks, their intricate patterns shine brilliantly as the morning sun passes through each transparent strand of silk. As I move between the stalks, the webs accumulate until my clothing takes on a crystalline sheen. The TL has come forward and tugs at my shirt to get my attention. With wide eyes, he points below into the shadows of the streambed; partially hidden beneath a few cut banana leaves are a number of scattered fuel drums. Kneeling beside me, the TL removes his web-covered bush hat and listens attentively; his bright yellow hair, matted from sweat, is caked with green grease paint in a feeble camouflage effort. Behind, I hear the coded position of the fuel drums being sent to the relay. Avoiding the fuel cache, we continue on along the ridge; sweat pours from us as our breathing becomes fast and furious, my stomach twists into tight knots of nausea as I reluctantly search for the unseen enemy. Each forced step that I coax from the legs that have become numb from torrential blasts of adrenaline becomes a terrifying labor that carries me closer to my destiny.

Somewhere below, on the bamboo-choked slope of the ridge, voices emerge. Without being told, the veteran grenadier is already moving toward the safety of a deep crater; from there he will provide covering fire as we work our way to him. Like an animal that has suddenly encountered a deadly trap, I back slowly away from the danger; no longer breathing ... I hear my heart pounding in my ears. The TL whispers loudly for me to move toward the crater; he is on one knee behind a termite mound, his rifle aimed into the thick mass of bamboo that separates me from the invisible enemy. I turn and quickly move toward him while constantly watching his wild scanning eyes; I pray that they do not focus on a single object.

Waiting for me to cover the short distance, he suddenly unleashes a volley of rifle fire. A brilliant uninterrupted stream of golden brass, flashing in the morning sun, is sent skyward from his M-16 until the magazine is spent; boiling gray smoke pours from the entire length of the barrel as oil, dew and spider webs are burned from the hot steel. In a flash, he has reloaded and sends another magazine into the bamboo wall. I do not turn to look at his target; instead, I sprint past him toward the rest of the team and the safety of the crater. The firing has stopped just as quickly as it began; only now do I feel the sting in my right knee and the warmth that flows from the wound. Again we hear the voices that have now become filled with the same panic that dominates our speech; the TL is asking for an immediate extraction as well as air support. Without looking at the wound, I take the battle dressing from its place in the cargo pocket of my jungle trousers and tie it tightly around the knee. The TL pauses from the message he is sending and asks if I can run. Without answering I bend the knee to show him that it is not broken; we are ordered to break contact and evade the enemy.

Before we are able to flee, the firing begins again from different directions; we are trapped, there is no longer a way out, the crater has been enveloped. The noise of the firefight grows until the distinct sounds of AK and M-16 fire blend into a single uninterrupted ripping blast; the grenadier punctuates the blast with the sharp detonations of high explosive rounds sent in volleys into the hidden enemy grunts. As steel jacketed bullets rip into the nearby banana trees, an eruption of green fibers, sticky with sweet sap, sprays across the crater. At the very bottom of the crater, covered with the sticky pulp, the radio operator tries to communicate with the relay; the noise of the firefight is deafening, he holds the handset tight to his ear while covering the exposed ear with his free hand. Now there is no fear, torrential waves of adrenaline flow into our blood as we

NVA base camp near Laos in early summer, 1968. The camp had been abandoned shortly before our 4-man team discovered it. Shallow mass graves from the heavy bombing of the area were found along with rice, equipment, weapons and documents. Moments after this photo was taken, our team received automatic rifle fire and was extracted by helicopter; we received two minor casualties.

react, countering each move made by the maneuvering enemy; to our advantage, our adversary has yet to determine the size of our unit. The Asian voices in the bamboo have become desperate as commands are sent through the din of rifle fire; the thick obstruction of bamboo impedes their ability to coordinate their advance. Though the enemy is very close, they remain unseen; in this bush war there is seldom a visible target for either of the combatants. The fighting is about fire superiority, sending a greater volume of fire into the enemy than he is able to return. We fire blindly into the thick vegetation toward the blasts and flashes that come from hidden rifles, never to know if our rounds have found their mark and never to know if we have killed. The firefight becomes intimate as I concentrate on my area of responsibility; it is now a personal duel between my rifle and those that are trying to reach and over-run the muddy hole. For me, the fighting is reduced to the one third of the crater's circumference that I am assigned to defend. Although I hear the firing from the TL and the grenadier coming from behind, I am immersed into my own private affair with the deadly wall of bamboo and banana trees directly in front of my position. The radio operator, sitting alone in the bottom of the crater, is unable to communicate verbally with those of us defending the rim because of the constant overwhelming noise. He can only point to the sky as the relay notifies him that the AO is on the way; directly above the earsplitting clatter of rifle fire, we hear the Phantoms cross the sky. With the arrival of the jets we know that the fighting will become more vicious; the enemy must close quickly before the napalm is sent into the skirmish.

I hear the impact of an AK round as it finds the grenadier; he is blown from the rim of the crater. Still clutching the handset to his ear, the radio operator crawls to the stricken Marine and searches frantically for the wound. We are relieved when told that the round passed through the Marine's pack from side to side; he is alive but stunned. Now it is just the TL and me defending the rim; grenades and magazines are tossed up to us. The firing finds new fury as the stubborn enemy continues to maneuver, searching for a weak spot in our defense. The radio operator has made contact with the AO, the tiny spotter plane that seems so vulnerable is circling above the fighting and asks for our bright orange panel to be displayed in the bottom of the crater; he will direct the jets into their run once we are identified. From his vantage point above the firefight, the observer is able to count a number of casualties that our rifles and grenades have inflicted. The enemy troops continue to close but seem reluctant to expose themselves by rushing the rim of the crater, perhaps they fear the tiny plane and the hell that he can unleash. The AO fires a white phosphorus rocket to mark the target and the first of the heavily laden Phantoms streaks by extremely low. The huge jet is on us with no warning, a deafening roar from the massive engines trails far behind; the first container of napalm is released ... clear liquid streams from the bright silver canister as it tumbles end over end to the earth. As the napalm bomb disappears into the banana trees below, a huge wall of fire erupts nearby; the heat fills the crater and the oxygen is sucked from us. The jet blasts the trees with his afterburners, climbing to escape the rifle and machine gun fire; immediately, another attacks from a different direction, releasing a burst of cannon fire that strikes the earth like a jackhammer. The enemy grunts seem confused and are becoming disorganized; perhaps their command element has been incinerated. The jets continue to make runs as we hear the first familiar sound of helicopter turbines coming from the east. The AO tells us that the enemy seems to be seeking cover along the ridge; he wants to extract us immediately, as our presence impedes the effectiveness of the attacking Phantoms ... we are eager to comply with their wishes. The lead troopship wants smoke to mark our position ... a yellow smoke grenade is tossed within a few feet of the crater's rim. Immediately, we are taken by surprise as the lead chopper approaches the crater without hesitation. The twin rotors drive the bright yellow smoke into the burning bamboo, where it mixes with the black smoke from the napalm; the swirling mixture closes over us, blocking the view of our extraction from the circling AO. With both gunners sending volleys of .50-caliber fire into the burning bamboo, the big helicopter crosses the crater, casting a dark shadow over us; I can nearly touch the underbelly and for an instant I am sure that he will lurch and crush us. As the pilot hovers the troopship into position to pick us up, the left rear set of tandem tires drags across the rim, causing a section of the crater to collapse onto the radio operator. The TL and I drag the half buried Marine from the collapsed crater. Without the PRC-25, he emerges choking and spitting, covered with a thick layer of red dirt that sticks to the glue-like sap from the bullet-shredded banana trees. The TL prevents the team from searching for the buried radio, there is no time; it must be abandoned. The powerful rotors fan the flames that the napalm ignited and as we scramble from our damaged fortress, the flaming bamboo bursts into an inferno. The TL helps the stunned grenadier while the dirt-covered radio operator and I provide covering fire. We hear only the engines; we are sucked into the all-too-familiar vacuum of hot exhaust and flame, again the world moves in slow motion. The chopper does not stop rolling across the scorched bamboo and flattened banana trees; we struggle onto the pitching ramp and pull one another into the seemingly safe haven of thin aluminum. Suddenly, we are in a steep climb to escape the enemy gunners; through the open cargo ramp we see the earth erupting into red dirt geysers that spew toward the sky as "snake-eye" bombs are sent into the small, insignificant crater that we fought so hard to defend.

As we climb above the hell below, I remove the sweat soaked bandage from my leg; it is caked with the sticky pulp from the banana trees. The TL slits the leg of the jungle trouser with his Ka-Bar in order to examine the wound. Under the faded green material, the blood has stopped and has dried in long streams of red gelatin that snake down my leg, disappearing into the frayed jungle boot. We clean the wound with canteen water; beneath the red dirt and dried blood we find only a tiny puncture that hardly seems able to have allowed so much blood to flow.

We fly to LZ Stud to be de-briefed; the grenadier and I are taken into a deep, cool bunker to a host of waiting Corpsmen. They clean the wound and after prodding into the tiny hole, a small piece of shiny copper-colored metal is removed from just beneath the skin. It is a sharp piece of metal jacket; the bullet must have disintegrated upon impact with the ground and the fragment ricocheted into my knee. The grenadier has a sprained back; the rifle round ripped through his pack and passed through cans of rations and canteens of water. The thick canvas straps tore into his shoulders and as he was twisted violently, the muscles in his back were wrenched and torn. I am told to return to the de-briefing. The grenadier will be sent south where he will be x-rayed; within days he will return to the team.

Our mission was accomplished when we heard the truck engine in the early morning darkness; the discovery of the fuel cache verified the enemy presence. Each of us agrees with the TL that we should have left the area after finding the drums; there was no reason to continue our search. At the completion of the de-briefing, we are returned to Dong Ha for further assessment. After drawing overlays and answering an endless barrage of tedious questions, we are told that an eight-man "Stingray" team from Battalion Recon will be inserted into the same area the following day. The TL thinks we should travel to their base at Quang Tri and meet with them; they are being sent to destroy the enemy that we found, our team feels responsible for their welfare. We are denied transportation to Quang Tri and told that the Battalion team will have access to the information we gathered. We return to our hooch to clean our weapons; the TL cleans the grenadier's M-79. The Corpsmen have assured us that he will return soon.

In my mind I picture our Battalion brothers searching to the west of the smoldering ridgeline; their killing pack will soon find their prey. Always unseen … always unheard, their heavily armed column moves swiftly and cautiously toward Laos and the setting sun, while the flowing shadow that emerges slowly and deliberately from the massive wall threatens to absorb their souls into the stone that has been turned black by the blood of martyrs.

14

The Trail

I am now Team Leader ... it isn't my idea ... I have never wanted the responsibility. My friend is our Platoon Sergeant and has asked me to take one of the teams; I refuse but he insists and tells me that there is no one else to lead the team. I am reminded that I am on my second tour and now have more bush time than anyone else in the unit. It is my turn to step forward and shoulder some of the leadership load; reluctantly, I accept the unwanted position. Feeling suddenly alone, I ask my friend to help me through the initiation of leadership by coming along on this patrol ... he agrees.

I form a four-man team consisting of grenadier, radio operator, assistant team leader and myself. The Sergeant will be the point and ATL for this patrol; together we go over to the office to pick up our patrol order and to be briefed. The order states that we will go out to LZ Stud by helicopter and report to the General's bunker. We are told that he will advise us concerning our actual mission. After we meet with him, we will be inserted some ten kilometers south of LZ Stud, deep within the Da Krong Valley. We are to search for an infiltration trail that the enemy is suspected of building. If we are able to locate the trail, we are to observe and report any enemy activity moving along it. We are not to make contact with the enemy unless the opportunity arises to take a prisoner. This is a bad area that we are going into; I am worried about my ability to lead the others. After the Sergeant and I return with the order, I call the team together to discuss the patrol; I try to act the part of leader but it does not work, the façade is paper-thin. Gathered around an old wooden ammo crate that serves as a table, we carefully study each detail of the four-grid-square recon zone that we will patrol for the next five days.

As I look at the worn map, the names of rivers and mountains that I know so well beckon to me; the names are engraved deep into my memory. I think of other patrols into the Da Krong many months before and think of the teammates that I arrived in Vietnam with that left when their thirteen months were completed; I think of those that left early in their tours ... some wounded ... others dead. Letters that I receive from my departed comrades tell of wives and college and new cars, but between the lines, I am able to detect a certain longing, not a desire to return to the Annam Cordillera but rather a longing to reunite with the piece of their youth that they left here. They want to be home, yet they want to remain attached to this far away land into which they invested so much of themselves. I have told them in letters that now our teams consist of only four men rather than the deadly eight-man "Stingray" teams that they remember, and I have told them of the replacements that came after they left ... how young they look and how old I feel.

My mind returns to the present and I designate who will carry the Claymore mines and who will carry the extra radio batteries. We have been issued a small VHF radio that is locked onto a specific frequency monitored by aircraft; we are amazed at its compact size. In order to increase our speed and stealth, I entertain the thought of leaving the M-79 grenade launcher behind. The idea is quickly dismissed as the names on the map summon terror-filled memories of close calls and narrow escapes; so often the survival of a team has depended on the lethal effectiveness of the weapon. I decide to divide the sixty rounds of 40mm grenades between the team, excluding the radio operator, who is burdened with the PRC-25. The Sergeant and I will each carry ten of the rounds and the grenadier will carry forty. I will carry the extra batteries for the primary radio and a Claymore. The Sergeant, who will be point, will carry the other Claymore, a machete, plasma and morphine. Each man will carry the usual bush gear and armament, M-16 with twenty magazines of eighteen rounds each and eight fragmentation grenades; in addition, there will be at least one smoke grenade per man. We determine that due to the availability of water, four canteens will be adequate. Each man carries rations to last for at least five days.

At daylight, we hitch a ride aboard a CH-46 re-supply chopper and fly directly to LZ Stud. We are not alone on the crowded helicopter; there are a number of Marines returning to the firebases after brief visits in the rear areas. Though they are wearing the new Marine Corps camouflaged jungle utility uniforms, their worn out boots are testament that these are not replacement troops. As we approach the jagged tooth of the Rockpile, the helicopter suddenly turns south following Route 9 into the pass toward Ca Lu. Soon the lush green of the Truong Son encounters the impassable rows of razor wire that encompass the slash of red scar that is LZ Stud. Having been scraped clear of vegetation by the onslaught of bulldozers, the dramatic contrast that separates the ugly, barren outpost and surrounding rain forest is vivid; as thin streams of bright red dust drift through the ominous perimeter, from high above, the outpost resembles a bleeding wound.

After landing, we disembark and search for a place to escape the constant activity; the LZ is immersed into a swirling red cloud that is created by the constant approach and departure of turbine-powered rotors. Like hungry flies feeding on the open wound, helicopters swarm above the churning dust; most never land, instead they hover while red nylon cargo nets are hooked underneath their bellies. The nets are filled with rations, ammo, artillery rounds, water cans, body bags, razor wire, and sand bags. With the base at Khe Sanh now abandoned, anything that is needed to maintain the war along the Laotian border comes through LZ Stud. As one chopper leaves with its dangling cargo, another immediately takes its place for a share of the goods. In the shade of a bunker, we find shelter from the turmoil and drop our gear; there are other teams that will be inserted ahead of us. We kill time by studying our maps and double-checking and triple checking each item of equipment.

Marines from the outlying firebases are gathered around the LZ hoping to find a space aboard any chopper returning to Dong Ha … and … there are the dead. Wrapped in ponchos, they wait in a row on the far side of the dusty LZ; worn out jungle boots protrude from each of the green ponchos. The torn and frayed ponchos that are covered with red dirt flap wildly as blurred rotor blades violently fan the dusty LZ, a detail of Marines is transferring the dead into body bags; the war goes on. I realize that if I am wasted, the war will not pause; why have I entertained that notion in the past? If killed, I will suddenly become a plastic-wrapped bundle of non-priority cargo; I will wait on some lonely dust-choked LZ amid the many stacks and piles of crates, cans and pallets.

A Corporal approaches and asks us to come with him. We grab our weapons and gear and follow him as he leads us from the LZ and down into the bowels of a deep, cool bunker. He tells us that the General will be with us in one moment; we stand close to the wooden wall while nervously awaiting our host. I suggest to my friend, in a matter of fact manner, that since he is our Platoon Sergeant, he should be the one to deal with the General; he reminds me with a mischievous grin that I am the TL and it is my responsibility, then the grenadier and radio operator laugh at my sudden misfortune. Dressed in a faded green undershirt and jungle utility trousers, the smiling General makes his entrance; we are immediately comfortable with him. He wears no insignia of rank, yet due to his confident bearing, he could never be mistaken for anything but a General. Summoning every ounce of courage, I introduce the members of our team; the general shakes each hand. Perhaps understanding that we are nervous, he draws laughter from us with colorful jokes that can only be interpreted by a fellow bush Marine. He offers us a can of soda and allows us to smoke. On a wall is a huge map; we can see the names of our sister teams scattered across the mountainous terrain, their recon zones outlined with the red and black from grease pencils. It is the biggest map that I have ever seen and the detail is flawless; outlined in bright red is the RZ that waits for us, our team call sign is written near the square. After he has made sure that we are comfortable, he begins his briefing. He shows us where he wants our movement concentrated, perhaps he is fed up with secondhand information or perhaps he is cutting out all of the middlemen that have a habit of discarding the hard earned intelligence the recon teams gather; he makes us feel as though we are finally being listened to. The General only wants to find the enemy supply trail so that he can destroy it; the trail is killing the General's grunts. A sudden feeling of significance overwhelms our ragged little band; the General has entrusted our team with a task that is obviously very important, and we are eager to help him. Before leaving us, he reiterates that we are not to engage the enemy and that he is counting on us to gather the information so desperately needed. I silently wish that he were going with us. He has a way of making me feel safe ... he knows how to lead people.

We leave the cool depths of the bunker and make our way across the hot, dusty LZ to the waiting helicopter; as the CH-46 climbs, we enjoy the rush of cool wind through the windows. I look below for the bunker that we just left, but we are moving too fast; below us the LZ is hidden beneath a red, dusty haze. As the helicopter flies toward our destiny, I hold an M-16 magazine in the air as a signal to the others and shove it into the empty magazine well of my rifle, then I pull the bolt to the rear and feed a round into the bright chrome chamber and strike the bolt assist with my open palm; each team member does the same. We are locked, loaded and flying south toward the Laotian border and once again, encroaching into the lair of Ho Mang Chua.

The CH-46, designated ET-3 or "Echo Tango-Trey," follows the winding Da Krong River along the floor of the valley. Below us, the terrain is the familiar, jagged, dark green ridges and massive grottos of triple canopy jungle. Often, I wonder if we are the very first people to venture into these remote areas. The gunners, manning their fifty-caliber Brownings, jack rounds into the chambers, they know that we are entering a very bad area. The flight seems long for ten kilometers; occasionally I compare my map with the topographical features below in order to judge the amount of flying time left to the RZ. Along the ridgelines there is tremendous devastation from B-52 attacks; the destruction will not linger, soon the jungle will replenish itself. In the distance I see the gray smoke from explosions, perhaps it is the artillery support for another of our teams—or perhaps our enemy. I silently wonder how many engagements with the enemy are occurring this instant in our area of operation. As I look into the vast, tangled grottos below, our efforts seem so insignificant; our brief intrusion is less than a fleeting instant in the violent history of the Truong Son.

As we near our insertion point, I go forward to show the pilot my map. He points below and then to a place on the map; I nod in agreement and move back to the other team members. They each have their heads out the round windows searching the ground for movement. I have told them that if they see anything, anything at all, to fire at it and we will abort the patrol. Everyone is nervous; we strain our eyes trying to see through the thick canopy that rushes just beneath the helicopter. Looking through the round window, I can see the gun ships making strafing runs around the LZ that the pilot has picked for the insertion. Off to the left, the sister ship is staying with us. I am shaking with fear; I have been inserted countless times yet I am still afraid. What will we encounter on the LZ? If we are assaulted, will our tiny four-man team be able to repel the enemy? Why didn't I bring more M-79 rounds? The adrenaline is pumping in my veins; unanswered questions accumulate in my mind, adding to the turmoil created by panic. I know that my lips are trembling and I look away from the others; I am ashamed that I am afraid. I will hide my secret from them, knowing that I am not as strong as they want me to be; I don't want to be the leader.

The chopper is making its run for the LZ; the cargo ramp is wide open and through the open portal we see the jungle that is coming up fast. I can see individual things now, peaceful waterfalls and beautiful ferns. The pilot is committed; he is on a direct path to the LZ. I signal the team to move back onto the cargo ramp. We will all jump out in one group as the chopper hovers low over the hostile landing zone. The gunners constantly scan the jungle below, the heavy machine guns traversing. To combat our fear, the team engages in an exaggerated horseplay on the pitching cargo ramp. Now is the exciting time that becomes a vivid slow motion dream; my body is numb from the massive amount of adrenaline that continues to enter my bloodstream. We are close, now the musty smell of the jungle is in the helicopter; it mixes with the smell of turbine exhaust creating the familiar smell that we will never forget. Soon the quiet will come and it will remain quiet for the next five days. We will never talk above a whisper for the duration of the patrol; fear will transform itself into awareness and our senses will once again become those of hunter and hunted. The grenadier is praying and crosses himself; I call everyone farther back onto the ramp. The jungle is coming up faster; the chopper strains and vibrates as if it is reluctant to go any lower, as if knowing that the enemy may be waiting. The engine noise is deafening, the gunners scan, I am shaking with adrenaline … how will my life ever be exciting after this?

Suddenly, the radio operator fires his M-16 out the closest window. At the same instant both gunners open up with a hail of fifty-caliber fire. The chopper is shaking from the recoil of the heavy machine guns. Outside the opened ramp, anti-aircraft flak is coming at us; the explosions are working their way toward the opened ramp. When we are hit, the back of the helicopter comes apart. Hydraulic fluid gushes from ruptured tubing and the prop blast blows it into my eyes. Though it is obvious that the chopper is mortally wounded, the machine gun and automatic rifle fire continues from the aircrew and the recon team. The rear rotor has lost power and we are plunging toward the jungle. I see white flashes of 12.7mm machine gun tracers pass the window nearest to me. ET-3 is being ripped apart; she shudders as the tracers now pass through the thin fuselage. Shards of green aluminum are torn and ripped loose, becoming deadly projectiles; I see the jungle coming up fast. As we auto-rotate, the pilot is fighting to prevent the doomed helicopter from inverting. When we hit, I am thrown into the fuselage. The front rotor is wrapping around the crippled chopper and pieces of blade come through the thin aluminum like cleaving axe heads. ET-3 bounces violently each time the rotor blades strike the trees and the ground. I smell fuel and wait for the explosion, it does not come; total quiet is upon us. For a brief second that seems an eternity no one moves or speaks, we hear only the distant sound of rifle fire coming toward us. The ramp is clogged with dirt and tree limbs, we can't get out back there. Everyone begins to scramble out the windows; fuel is all over the crash site.

I am unable to find the grenadier; was he thrown out as we came down? I move toward the ramp but slip on the hydraulic fluid. The floor of the helicopter is littered with spent machine gun and rifle brass. The gunners are removing the machine guns and I move forward to help them. The port gunner turns to me and tells me to get out because the fuel is probably going to blow. Quickly, I climb through a window and fall head first into the brush. My clothing is soaked with the fuel. Up forward the port gunner is struggling to remove his heavy machine gun; I crawl forward through the thick brush to help him. I grab the red-hot barrel to help him lift, and though I wear leather gloves, I still have to use my bush hat for insulation from the hot steel. I ask where the grenadier is and no one knows. Was he blown out of the chopper when the round hit us? I search frantically, then return to the ramp and begin to dig under it. Sweat is pouring from me as I dig. Suddenly, he appears from the other side of the chopper. The Sergeant chews him out for not answering up when we called his name.

The enemy grunts are cautiously coming to us while overhead, Hucy gun ships are making rocket and machine gun runs around the downed chopper. The pilot forms up his crew and is in contact with the sister CH-46 that is orbiting overhead. We are advised to move down to the river and they will try to get us out. The enemy, signaling with rifle fire ... is getting closer; searching for survivors, they try to draw fire from the crash site. I pass the word for none of my team to fire unless they absolutely have to; they already know this and suddenly, I feel stupid for telling them. We begin to move down into the steep ravine to the rocky Da Krong River. I tell the Sergeant that we may get wasted in the riverbed and I want to move uphill to be extracted. The Sergeant, agreeing with the aircrew, thinks the riverbed offers the best opportunity for an extraction. As we discuss the matter, the aircrew is already moving toward the river, without hesitation we find a place in the column. Using our VHF radio, the pilot is in contact with the orbiting sister-ship ... I think that I smell bacon frying ... I look behind me and see that it is the starboard gunner's hand. He has a grip on the hot machine gun barrel. His hand is smoking but he shows no apparent pain. I take his hand from the barrel and see that it is badly blistered;

apparently he feels no pain due to the massive amount of adrena-line that is pumping through him. I give him my bush hat to wrap around the hot barrel. The pilot has the gunners remove the trig-gers from the guns and bury them in the mud. He knows that we will never be able to get the heavy machine guns out.

As we approach the river, the recon team moves to the head of the column in order to provide covering rifle fire. As the team approaches the rocky riverbed, we realize that we have entered a well-traveled path. There are fresh footprints; some still have water running into them. I call the Sergeant up and we realize that it is a covered trail ... we have found the General's trail. I am amazed that they can accomplish such a feat; for how many kilometers is the trail covered with the thatched roof? It seems an impossibility to build such a structure. The enemy has shot us down on top of the trail that we were sent to find. The pilot continues to talk with the choppers above, figuring out how to get in here to get us. They are his friends; they won't leave without him ... it is their code of honor.

The rifle fire is approaching. Looking down the stream, I think I see an NVA soldier run across. From the breast pocket of my jacket I take out my map, compass, shackle sheet and codebook and after digging a hole with my Ka-Bar, I bury them deep in the black river mud. With dark approaching, I don't think that we are going to get out of this place alive. The pilots are the prize that the enemy troops want. The rest of us will be shot. The North Vietnamese don't take grunt prisoners; each of us knows that.

The pilot tells us that the sister ship is going to try to get in and wants a red smoke. Someone passes the canister up to him and he throws it all the way across the river. I hear the chopper com-ing down the ravine. Tracers are chasing it and her gunners are firing. Now I am sure that if we do get aboard, we will never get out of the ravine. I tell the team to remove the bolts from their weapons; then the rifles are tossed into the swirling water. I throw my Colt as far as possible into the rock-strewn river; I do not want the pistol captured. The grenadier smashes the M-79 against a tree and destroys the sight; after breaking the weapon down he tosses the pieces into the rapids. For a brief moment, the weapon seems suspended in an eddy; its glistening, wooden stock stands upright in the whirlpool before it slides to the bottom. We are throwing our gear into the river as the chopper suddenly appears. The engine noise is deafening and the rotor wash engulfs us like an icy cyclone; we have to bend forward to move against the force. The typhoon wind from the rotors is unable to destroy the thatched roof of the trail; I am once again amazed. Behind us, the rifle fire is coming closer. This part of the river is a rapid; it is impossible for the chopper to set down in the raging water. There is a large boulder nearby so I climb onto it. My jungle jacket has been blown open and as it violently flaps, it is beating me in the face; I bend forward to prevent being blown from the smooth boulder. Incredibly, while in a hover, the pilot backs the ramp to me. Reaching up, I grab the slick aluminum, I have no strength left, the adrenaline has stripped me; somehow I manage to get a leg in and then the crew chief has my belt. He drags me onto the slippery ramp; as the chopper jerks and thrusts, I claw at the aluminum. I want to crawl forward and find a place to hide from this madness but the crew chief is struggling with the next man ... I help him with the others. I think that rounds are hitting the chopper and jagged pieces of green aluminum are beginning to litter the deck. The deafening engine noise will cover the steady reports from the enemy machine guns. Held in the hover, the helicopter is being tortured, and like a wounded panther, her turbines are screaming louder now. We work frantically, dragging the wet Marines onto the pitching ramp. I glance through the nearest window to my right and think that I see the fleeting shapes of enemy troops moving cautiously up the rapids towards us ... I can't be sure. Perhaps they are waiting for the port gunner to open up with his .50-caliber, not knowing that the gunner is not at his station because he is helping to get the others aboard. When the last man is pulled onto the ramp, the chopper crew begins to fight their way out of the deep ravine. As the fifty-calibers hammer at the steep walls of jungle that form the ravine, smoke pours from the hot barrels. I have found a revolver on the littered floor and fire blindly at the green blur of the ravine. The engines strain to escape the enemy gunners ... we wait for the anti-aircraft fire that will bring us down. Suddenly, we are free of the ravine and climbing fast. The machine guns cease-fire; the helicopter is filled with the smell of burned oil.

A mortally wounded ET-3. The helicopter, flown by Mike Mullen, was hit with 37mm and 12.7mm anti-aircraft fire during an attempt to insert our team into the Da Krong Valley. With a large force of NVA troops approaching, Ron Kittren took this last photo of the "Gallant Lady." She was destroyed moments after this photo was taken. "Sky Hawk" jets from Chu Lai dropped napalm on her to prevent the enemy from plundering the wreckage. This photograph received water damage during our rescue from the Da Krong River. Although critically low on fuel, Richard Herberg and his brave crew ignored the anti-aircraft fire and flew into the steep river valley to pick us up (courtesy of Ron Kittren).

The crew chief comes back to retrieve his revolver and passes around a pack of cigarettes; the aircrew and recon team are piled on top of one another in a heap. The engine noise is deafening yet comforting; we are alive and owe our lives to both of the aircrews. The deep ravine grows smaller as we climb, until it blends and finally disappears into the plush, green peaks that line the Da Krong River.

We return to LZ Stud and are once again brought to the General's bunker. There has been no time to thank the brave crew for getting us out and no time to thank the crew of the doomed chopper for making the controlled crash; it will be thirty-three years before we meet again. We have only been gone for a short period but we have accomplished our mission. The General is ecstatic, cold beer is passed around; as he looks on, we pinpoint the trail on his map. A flight of A-4 Sky Hawks from Chu Lai, their radio call sign being "Hell Borne," have destroyed Echo Tango-3. Air strikes with "snake and nape" have completed the task that our hidden enemy began. The aircrew and recon team is alive and safe; it is a happy time in the bunker. The General wants to know the pilot's name that got us out; we only know the number of the chopper. There is talk of decorations but we don't want to hear about it; my team and the brave aircrews are alive ... that is all I care about.

Before dark, we return to Dong Ha, where we are once again debriefed. The office is a shambles as our Company prepares, reluctantly, to relocate to Thon Ai Tu where we will join with Battalion Recon. Office clerks drag boxes of documents outside to be burned; our unit's history is being destroyed. Reports and overlays from the briefings and debriefings of patrols filled with heroic actions by brave Marines are tossed in a pile and burned. There will be no reminder of what has happened here and in time, our efforts will be forgotten.

Within the noise and turmoil of the office, a Lieutenant and a Staff Sergeant question us; we do not know either of the two. Perhaps they are new to the Company or perhaps they are from Battalion Recon; both are obviously new to Vietnam. There are no familiar Officers or Staff NCOs in the office; frantically my eyes search for one of our leaders to arrive and rescue us from the interrogation. The Staff Sergeant is upset that we have lost all of our gear. I explain that we were going to be overrun and I ordered the team to destroy everything. Then, my friend the Sergeant tries to explain but it all falls on deaf ears; non-combatants are chastising us. Everything that I buried in the black mud of the Da Krong Valley was "secret" and is now considered compromised. The VHF radio is missing and though I last saw the pilot with it, the assumption is that it is in the hands of the enemy. I am told how hard it was to get them and that they were merely on loan to us.

The Staff Sergeant attacks me verbally, I remain at attention yet I want to walk away; he has not earned the right to humiliate me ... he does not possess the eyes of a bush Marine. Next to me my friend is beyond caring and at times lashes out at the two of them; thinking that he will lunge, I hold the sleeve of his jacket. Our eyes are irritated from the fumes coming from our fuel-soaked uniforms; soaked with the fuel that should have been the source of our funeral pyre. I stare at the wall directly in front of me; beyond caring, I accept the humiliation. The Sergeant is allowed to leave but since I was the team leader, I am kept behind to draw an overlay. I explain that I have no accurate idea of where we crashed; I remind the Staff Sergeant that I buried my map in the mud, and his verbal assault gains momentum. Having taken enough abuse, I counterattack by recommending they contact the General over at LZ Stud and debrief him. The office becomes quiet; the tone of my voice has crossed the line that borders on insubordination. Again I am attacked verbally; I feel the tears that are welling in my eyes from both the fuel and the frustration. My eyes scan the office, searching for a friendly face; I wish the General were here, hearing the hell that is being rained on one of his boys, I know that he would protect me. We have accomplished our mission. No one was killed or wounded, it was a good effort. I had felt very proud and happy in the bunker drinking the General's beer, but now I am shattered and demoralized.

Told to leave, I meet the Sergeant outside and together we meander slowly toward the sanctuary of our hooch. We curse each of the jackals that attacked us. I tell the Sergeant that if I knew an enemy forward observer, I would plot an artillery mission and help him blow the sons-of-bitches to hell. My friend, never to be outdone, adds that he would actually adjust the enemy fire until the office was bracketed; I am unable to top that. The anger and frustration suddenly turn to laughter as the Sergeant mimics the green Staff Sergeant. We can only shake our heads in disbelief; "it don't mean nothing." Tomorrow we will draw new equipment and prepare for the next patrol; perhaps when we return they will be gone.

Within the safe haven of our plywood lair, the Sergeant produces a bottle of "stateside" whiskey. Our team will burn the chill of the Da Krong from our bones and calm our nerves from the verbal assault. The Gunny has come to talk to us; though he will never tell us, we know that he is upset at the treatment we received. I ask him about my insubordination toward the two strangers, he tells me to forget the incident; it has already been taken care of. He congratulates our team for a successful mission. The Gunny is a stand up guy; we ask him to stay and drink with us … he does.

15

The Border; into Laos

Our unit has been ordered to relocate from our base at Dong Ha to Thon Ai Tu, located just north of Quang Tri City along *la rue sans joie* ... "the Street Without Joy." Though we are told that we are merely being removed from the fan of enemy artillery, each of us suspects that our tiny unit, the Third Force Recon Company, is finally being completely absorbed into the larger Third Recon Battalion. Though we feel a strong kinship with the highly decorated battalion, perhaps the finest battalion to ever serve in Vietnam, we are reluctant to lose our independence. *Thon Ai Tu* means, roughly, "Orphan Boy Village." For our little band, the name seems appropriate.

My friend, the Sergeant, has a vast supply of contraband liquor hidden under our hooch. Returning from a trip to Da Nang with my radio operator, who was recently demoted to PFC, the two renegades produced case after case of quart bottles from stolen mailbags. The liquor traveled north to Dong Ha aboard a C-130 under the guise of the U.S. Mail; a priority cargo.

The move to Quang Tri has presented a few problems, mainly, how to relocate the Sergeant's inventory undetected. We have reserved a jeep and trailer at the cost of a mere two bottles; the jeep is normally reserved for officers, so it is doubtful we will be bothered along the way to Ai Tu. When we move, the Sergeant will be in the bush north of the Rockpile with our sister team; he has left

the relocation of his goods in my charge. This will be his first insertion by helicopter since being shot down a few days before.

By mid-morning the jeep and its trailer have been loaded and
sit ready to travel the 7.5 kilometers south along Route 1 to Ai Tu,
where we will find the green canvas tent that will become our new
lair. Our plywood home sits empty; though the hooch is perhaps a
mere two years old, the harsh Asian weather and North Vietnamese
rockets have sent the ravaged hut into a state of disrepair. It is
difficult to abandon our sanctuary where, for countless times, having returned from the Truong Son, we rested and healed while
preparing for the next hunt. Here we shared every possession and
learned the true meaning of the word ... family. Beneath the shrap-
nel-perforated tin roof our team became brothers and swore alle-
giance, not to America, nor Vietnam, but to the pack.

As we assure ourselves that nothing is being left behind, the
word is passed that a team is in heavy contact and is asking for an
immediate extraction; it is our sister team. Gathered around a radio,
we have found the frequency; the sounds of continuous gunfire
come from the attached speaker. A strained voice that is filled with
pain gives a med-evac number; he is asking for blood. I cringe as
I recognize the voice and the number; both belong to my friend.
Although severely wounded, he has taken charge of the radio, perhaps to allow the radio operator the freedom to help fight the
assaulting enemy. The team is surrounded and facing a vastly superior force. An AO is over them and is bringing jets into the battle;
from his vantage point high above, he sees enemy bodies all along
the hill, the little team is making the enemy pay dearly. Once again
they ask for blood and the extraction; their supply of ammo is running low. For those of us gathered around the radio listening, as
our comrades fight to survive, we are frustrated that we cannot help;
a flood of relief overcomes our compound when we hear that the
team has been extracted. I load my team into the jeep with all of
our earthly possessions and with the contraband liquor well hidden
in the trailer, the driver speeds toward Delta-Med, where we will
meet the extracted team.

The Sergeant has taken a 7.62mm through the leg from an
AK; we wait for him to come out of surgery. It is the first time that

I have returned to Delta-Med since my bout with malaria in nearly a year; there have been many improvements made during that time. A Corpsman tells us to follow him through a maze of plywood corridors that smells of strong antiseptic; the brilliance of the fluorescent lighting enhances the sterile atmosphere of the hospital. The Sergeant is in a comfortable bed with clean white sheets. Though weak and dazed, he is smiling as bottles of whole blood flow into his arm. Still smeared with green and black grease paint, his face is in harsh direct contrast to the background of the sterile white pillow case; in spite of his condition, he wants to know about the liquor. I tell him that it is just outside in the jeep; he is pleased that his goods are safe. When I ask how he was wounded, he begins the story by telling me that they were inserted into the wrong LZ; what would normally create a problem probably saved their lives.

After moving a few hundred meters to the intended LZ, they found that it was covered with bamboo poles that held anti-tank mines some ten feet off of the ground. Had the pilot landed on the correct LZ, the helicopter would have detonated one of the powerful mines, killing everyone aboard. Establishing a tiny perimeter along the edge of the LZ, the team began to disarm the mines. Noticing that one of the mines had a piece of Chinese communication wire attached, he cut it with his Ka-Bar; suddenly the cut wire began to snake away from him into a pile of logs. As he searched the logs for the enemy grunt that was retrieving the wire, from behind, he heard the metallic click of an AK selector. He turned to face an enemy soldier standing a mere ten feet away, dressed in complete battle gear with his rifle aimed in the direction my friend. The burst was wild, starting on the ground just in front of the Sergeant's feet, it passed between his legs all the while climbing until a round passed through the muscle of his upper thigh; had the selector on the weapon been set to semi-auto rather than auto, the Sergeant would not have survived. After firing, the soldier quickly moved into the brush to reload, only to be followed closely by a grenade; the soldier's helmet and bits of bloody tissue covered the LZ. From down the slope came the assault, the fighting was fierce throughout the day. The Sergeant begins to drift away, no longer able to combat the deep sleep that comes with shock and medication. The Corpsman tells us that we have to leave; our friend is being sent to Da Nang and from there he will travel on to a Naval Hospital in Japan. Moving closer to the drifting Sergeant, I ask what I am to do with the liquor; with a weakening voice he tells me to hide it well, he will return in a few days. Without my friend seeing him, the Corpsman silently shakes his head while looking me in the eye. My friend will not be coming back; it will be many long years before we meet again. Suddenly I feel totally alone and in danger.

After moving into our tent, our four-man team is briefed for a patrol along the Laotian border; once again, we will be operating beyond the range of artillery support. The six-square-kilometer recon zone that we are to patrol is only six kilometers due south of where we were recently shot down aboard ET-3. As the patrol order is read, I plot the boundaries on my map and see that the Laotian border runs diagonally through the two bottom grid squares, from NW to SE; at least one-fourth of the six grid squares are inside Laos. I ask the friendly Lieutenant reading the order how I am to move my team, and he tells me to pick my own insertion LZ and to move using my own discretion. The dominant terrain feature within the area is Hill 765, of which the razor-ridged summit is at least five hundred meters within Laos. It offers an excellent vantage point to observe the surrounding valleys in both Vietnam and Laos. Half of the six-square-kilometer RZ is hidden under thick, triple canopy rain forest that blankets the mountains. Down the steep slopes, the canopy gives way to high, green elephant grass that blends with thick stands of golden bamboo in the valley floors. Only three kilometers to the east of our eastern boundary sits Hill 850, or Nui Giang Gio.

We must assume that the massive mountain has enemy forward observers that will watch our insertion. With this in mind, we will be inserted a full kilometer or more down the steep northeastern slope of Hill 765, where our LZ will be bordered by thick, canopied jungle. The canopy will conceal our movement up the steep slope. I bring to the Lieutenant's attention that due to the harsh terrain, the unrealistic six grid squares that we are assigned are much too vast for our team to cover. He agrees and suggests we find an observation post that will allow us to cover the entire RZ visually. I realize

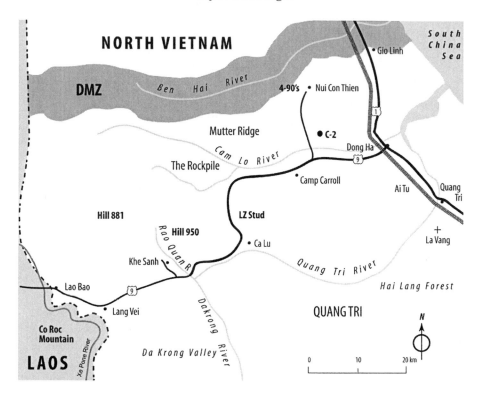

The northernmost section of Northern I Corps Tactical Zone; here the war was fought along the Demilitarized Zone as well as the Laotian border. The Marines, sailors, airmen and soldiers that fought in this area faced fresh North Vietnamese troops that were supported by long range rocket and artillery fire from across the nearby borders. This area was also located at the very end of the long supply line; often there were shortages of equipment.

that we will not be told to either enter into or stay out of Laos; I will use my own discretion as they have advised.

Having received the briefing, we return to the tent that we now call home. I am reluctant to re-enter the border area, having been shot down there only days before. The team gathers around the map to plan our movement. We are lost without our friend the Sergeant. Everyone hopes that he will return soon, yet we know that he is probably gone for good. Though we will miss him, we are thankful that he has survived his tour of duty. The climb to the summit of Hill 765 will be very difficult due to the steep slope up to the ridgeline that runs from northwest to southeast. I estimate that the climb will take at least two full days, leaving just two days on the summit and then a day to locate an LZ for extraction. Water will be a factor since we will not move down to the valley floor where the streams are found. It has rained heavy in the mountains so there should be plenty of flooded bomb craters. If we are unable to locate water, I will request an extraction and hope for the best. We decide to take an extra Claymore in the event we have to blast an LZ; the jungle is very thick and that will make an emergency extraction difficult. The Claymores should clear an area large enough to accommodate a CH-46; we have done this many times in the past. In addition to our food, water and ammo, there will be three Claymores, two radio batteries, and M-79 rounds; it will be a difficult climb.

At daylight, with our weapons and bush gear, we cross into the Battalion Recon area to listen to the insertion pilots receive their briefing. The senior pilot wants the area prepped with cannon before he will put us in; the call sign and radio frequency of the Phantoms that will be high above on station is given. The aircrews seem hesitant and concerned with this insertion; perhaps it is because they know all too well that if our team makes contact with the enemy, they will have to fly into an inferno of machine gun fire to make the extraction. Silently in my mind, I want the pilots to refuse this insertion; I have walked away from one crash but perhaps I will not be so lucky next time. The information given to the aircrews provides numerous locations of enemy units and anti-aircraft capabilities known to operate in and around our RZ. As the briefing progresses, I notice that the pilots are looking at each other and rolling their eyes as if in disbelief. Recent events have caused recon inserts to lose any shred of popularity they might have ever had with the helicopter crews.

Of the three teams that will be inserted into the Da Krong Valley, two are eight-man Stingray teams from Battalion Recon. They will be inserted along the valley floor nine kilometers to our northeast. We gather in the shade of the helicopters and wait for the pilots to arrive; the gunners are already feeding the linked belts into the fifty-caliber Brownings. The Stingray teams are burdened with a vast assortment of weapons and ammo. Each team has brought an M-60 machine gun with at least eight hundred rounds of belt ammo for each gun; the belts are divided among the team members. Unlike our four-man team, the eight-man teams will search out and engage any enemy they find. Our mission is to locate and observe the enemy while theirs, in addition to finding and observing, is pure attrition; they will simply and ruthlessly destroy the enemy with any means available. As the pilots arrive, we are told which chopper to board; we will fly to LZ Stud where the Stingray teams will remain while we are inserted.

The flight to LZ Stud crosses the razor-sharp ridges that form the backbone of the Truong Son. Below, the jungle and mountains rise to meet us; the familiar black-green peaks are slowly becoming enshrouded with the gray clouds that warn of the approaching monsoon season. It will soon be fall; my second fall. Soon my second winter will join the second spring and second summer that have come and gone. I enjoy the cool blast across my face and through my hair from the powerful rotors; with my head out the round window, I search the familiar mountains below for landmarks as the deafening noise from the engines pounds in my ears. I wonder about Con Ho, my protector from so many months before; perhaps he is close, safely hidden beneath the impenetrable triple canopy, quietly watching over me. Did he send me along this path? Will we meet again in this life or perhaps another? In the cold blast of the rotors, I wish my friend well.

We are approaching LZ Stud. The constant flow of men and cargo through the dusty LZ has not slowed since we were here a few days before. The helicopter hardly touches the ground and the eight men rush from the cargo ramp; suddenly, with no hesitation, we are climbing out of the swirling red dust. Escorted by two Huey gun ships and the second CH-46 sister ship, we fly due south toward the border, crossing the eighteen kilometers that separate LZ Stud from our recon zone. The flight is long and filled with the anxiety that accompanies all insertions. Ahead, we can see the shark-like Phantoms already diving to strafe the landing zone; streams of vapor streak from the sharp edges of their bomb-filled wings as they pull out of the steep dives. Bright flashes appear along the tree line and across the thick canopy as bursting cannon shells rip into suspected anti-aircraft emplacements, then white and orange funnels of fire erupt from the twin exhausts as afterburners propel them back to a safe altitude. Just as the lead Phantom pulls from his attack, the next rolls in, sending a burst of cannon fire along the deep ravine that may also harbor enemy gunners. I go forward to orient my map with the LZ, as seen through the eyes of the pilot. The cockpit is a vast array of gauges, lights, and switches that surround the pilot and co-pilot; though I have seen the multi-colored display many times before, I am still awestruck. The pilot takes the map from me and points below toward the distinct line that is created as the black-green canopy intrudes into the sea of light green elephant grass. As I look over his shoulder, he locates the selected LZ and with a pencil he lightly traces the line of the canopy onto my worn, rain-stained, plastic-wrapped map; the pilot nods his head, accepting my choice. The LZ that I requested looks good. It is very close to the triple canopy that will conceal our movement from enemy observers. Returning the map, he motions with a sweep of his free hand that he will approach the thick jungle from down the slope; because of the loud blasting engine noise, I am only able to respond with a nod.

Before moving back to the team, I hand the pilot a scribbled note. On a scrap of paper torn from the edge of my map I have written, "the service on this airline is terrible." The grinning pilot shares the crumpled and smudged note with the co-pilot that has control of the pitching chopper; then he glances over his shoulder toward me and holds a gloved middle finger in the air. The pilot places the scrap of paper into the zippered pocket of his sweat-soaked flight suit; I pat his shoulder as I turn to rejoin the team. I am told that they sometimes save the scribbled notes to show other pilots or perhaps send home.

Now the familiar nausea comes over me. My old companion fear is standing behind me; his long, thin, icy fingers probe into my guts, twisting and knotting. My breathing is rapid and shallow; there is no sweat, just the sick clammy feeling that accompanies panic. How many insertions is this for me? When did I stop counting? The number was once important, but now it means very little. This insertion is no different than my first nearly nineteen months before; each has been a gut-wrenching, adrenaline-driven, slow motion dream that has embedded the smell of JP-4 exhaust and humid jungle-musk deep into my soul, where it will always remain. Occasionally, the distinct smell that comes from heavy oil burning from a red-hot fifty-caliber barrel will also find its way into the potpourri of terror that my constant companion maintains.

The helicopter skims the tall grass, flying hard for the LZ; we are well below the dark canopy under which we will seek refuge. The team moves back to the ramp; there is no turning back now, the knots in my stomach constrict throughout my torso, rendering me breathless. A gun ship follows us into the grassy LZ; through the open ramp, we watch the sleek helicopter accelerate around our troopship and as he comes past the starboard windows, he unleashes a volley of rocket-fire into the tree line. The gunners carefully scan the fringe of canopy and the streambeds farther down the slope. From beneath my jungle jacket, the freshly issued Colt A-1 appears from the sweat soaked shoulder holster that is worn against my bare skin; I shove in a magazine and jack a round into the chamber. Then, with lightning speed, I pull the bolt to the rear on the new M-16 to test the extractor; the twirling rounds eject from the weapon in brilliant flashes of gold that disappear somewhere into the shadowed interior of the helicopter. My mind fills with cowardly thoughts of flight and escape, nausea floods my numb, trembling body that is frozen with terror. Realizing that there is no way out, I succumb to my companion and pray that the LZ is empty. Now we smell the sweet elephant grass and feel the furnace heat of the jungle; suddenly, without warning, the pilot stands the shuddering helicopter on end, stopping the forward progress, and at the same instant he swings the ramp close to the steep slope. In a fraction of a second, our team jumps blindly from the ramp into the sea of entangled green foliage, falling eight feet through the thick, matted elephant grass to the ground. The hot exhaust engulfs us as the pilot adds full power to escape the landing zone. He has executed a perfect feint to confuse any lurking mortar teams. As the helicopter climbs from the LZ, the wailing cry of turbine-powered engines is abruptly replaced by the familiar silence that once again swallows us. Quickly, having established radio contact with the relay, we flee the deadly LZ; tunneling our way through the sharp blades of humid elephant grass, our tiny column penetrates deep into the safety of the dark rain forest.

We move southwest as planned. The steep, vine-choked mountain is much thicker than we expected; for a brief instant I consider moving parallel to the wall of canopy, along the grassy slope to search for a passage through the snake-like vines. Instead, fearing the searching eyes that scan from the adjacent peaks, I decide to bore deeper into the protection of the triple canopy to hide and assess the situation. After moving a mere fifty meters through the steamy jungle, the point is already gasping for air; I hold the team up and move alone to a vantage point to observe the valley below. The valley is choked with thick elephant grass ten to twelve feet in height that is very difficult to traverse and offers little concealment from the enemy observers. Deciding to continue on to the summit, I signal the team up to explain the situation. None of the three want to go into the valley and risk being exposed to the mortars. Realizing that there is no easy way out, we begin the difficult climb up Hill 765 and into Laos.

The rain forest is very dark and the familiar sounds of monkeys and birds fill the canopy. The climb becomes a test of endurance and we stop to rest as often as possible. As late afternoon arrives the jungle is already becoming dark; it will be too dark to move when the afternoon sun fades to dusk. I want to search for a harbor site and stop early. Tomorrow will be much harder as we climb the steep wall that forms the razor-edged ridgeline. The team needs to rest and gather strength. Five hundred meters from the summit, we find a flat ledge that is approximately one hundred meters wide and perhaps twenty feet deep; as the steep slope rises vertically from the ledge it is a mass of tangled vines that grow to the clouds. Sweat is pouring from us. In the humid dark of the canopy, the mosquitoes have found their prey. We will sleep here with the wall behind us; we can go no farther. The three Claymores are set to cover a wide area; dark approaches as we eat. Looking up, we strain to find an end to the vast wall of jungle as each of us silently studies the climb that we will make the following morning; it seems almost impossible. The black of night arrives swiftly, and though peaceful, it is filled with the jungle sounds that prevent sleep. Soon, no one will sleep, as the animal sounds become increasingly human-like; as anxious hands clutch the "hellboxes" of the Claymores, strained eyes stare into the black void, searching frantically for the source. We are eager to move to the summit; if an emergency extraction is needed, it will have to be from the ridgeline, not on this steep wall of thick bush. Hours before daylight, the Claymores are collected and we begin the hard climb through the dark toward the summit.

The climb is challenging, much more so than the previous day. Excluding the radio operator, we alternate at point every fifty meters. As the mountain becomes steeper, we dig footholds into the wet dirt with our Ka-Bars. We move from tree to tree, vine to vine, hanging from one as we grab the next. There are no more ledges; it is a continuous, steep, vine-entangled wall with no relief. The radio operator holds the handset in the air and shakes his head; we have lost communication with the relay; the peaks have rendered us helpless. We have to reach the top as soon as possible.

The vertical climb is becoming almost unmanageable; each man struggles to make the next tree. Ahead we see clouds, the summit must be close; we have crossed the border into Laos. I motion to the radio operator and he shrugs his shoulders. Our communication is still intermittent. The summit is not far; I want to keep moving until we reach the top. The team is moving hard and fast, often someone loses their grip on a tree branch and slides down to the next tree. I think to myself that this climb will be impossible when the monsoon sets in. The radio operator motions to me that we are receiving transmissions; hanging from a vine with one hand, he sends an overdue situation report to the anxious relay.

As we reach the summit of the narrow ridgeline, we move into a thick stand of bamboo. Looking north through the breaks in the canopy, we are able to observe back into the valley where we were inserted. The majority of our RZ is visible from up here. To the south and west, into Laos, we have an even better view; some four kilometers west, the Vietnam border is once again encountered due to the meandering twists and turns of the ancient boundary. Through the dusk, we move westward across the steep ridgeline, searching for a defendable harbor site. The point has moved ahead to scout; he signals me forward and I move the other two men into a thick stand of vine-shrouded mahogany trees. Dark is approaching and from across the high forests and plateaus of Laos, the sunset is a dazzling spectacle. The disappearing rays, blazing with colorful hues, cast colors deep into the rain forest below. The colors create a tinted setting that constantly changes; at times our skin is red and then it becomes green or blue. The sun settles into the mountains of Thailand and as dark closes around the isolated team, like an old friend, Venus rises reassuringly in the western sky. We will keep two men awake at all times during the long night; one man is to watch into Vietnam, the other will look into Laos.

The night is long and dark. To the north, far in the distance, the sky is awash in the glow of illumination rounds. As the flares drift to earth under their parachutes, the black of night quickly absorbs the light, leaving no trace in the void. Occasionally a stream of orange machine gun tracers can be seen beneath the flares, we have no idea who is in that area. The faint flashes of artillery punctuate the balmy night and often the low rumblings of detonations arrive in the dark long after the flash has been absorbed back into the void. At night in the cloudy Annam Cordillera, it is impossible to determine where the jungle stops and the sky begins; the earth and heaven merge into a whole as the long darkness slowly progresses. Without sight, there is nothing but the black of night and the thoughts that wander through the mind. When the skies clear and the stars appear, the outline of the mountains is in sharp contrast to the endless array of scattered, glittering jewels. On this razor-edged ridgeline in Laos our four-man team seems so vulnerable, so small. When my watch comes, I am not alone; my companion reminds me with his long, icy fingers that he is always close. The jungle night could easily swallow us, leaving no trace; only the long umbilical cord of the PRC-25 prevents us from slipping into the dark unknown. At this very moment scattered across the mountains and valleys of the Annam Cordillera, isolated recon teams share the night, share the unknown, and feel the icy fingers. Always

The Annam Cordillera, August 1968. Looking west into Laos, the NVA infiltration routes are well hidden beneath the clouds.

searching, always scanning, always vigilant, none will ever use the word "alone" lightly again. Sitting in the liquid black ink we wait, while listening to the patterns of insect and animal sounds. We pray that the patterns remain constant while our scanning eyes are drawn to the east; anxiously they search for the glow that will summon the returning sun.

To the east beyond Hill 850, the sky is becoming pale; the stars have vanished, only the bright Morning Star remains. There has been little sleep through the long night; it is important that we relocate before the sun rises. The Claymores are collected and we move slowly from the harbor site, through the dew-soaked bamboo, into the early dawn. Our route is northwest along the long ridge; we will search for a new observation post. We have moved only a short distance when in the distance ... a rooster crows. Immediately, the team is hidden; a rooster can only mean that an enemy camp is near. Without being told, the radio operator is already sending the situation report to the relay; I decide to leave the mountain. We change direction northeast toward the steep slope. The point stops and signals the team to take cover. He wants me to come forward; I crawl through the wet elephant grass to reach him. Without speaking, he points into the brush; strung carefully through the grass are numerous strands of Chinese communication wire. The pale green wire must be connecting a number of field phones that are scattered along the ridge. Farther away, the rooster crows once again; adrenaline pumps into our bloodstreams bringing with it the familiar rapid, shallow breathing. The balance of the team crawls forward; the radio is once again sending. I want to reach the safety of the steep slope but we must change direction again. The wire seems to be running northwest to southeast; we will move due north. The slope is reached after a mere one hundred and fifty meters but we decide to move due east along the ridge using the thick jungle along the slope for concealment. The point has spotted movement to the right, south of us. There is no time to form a defensive perimeter; without artillery support the team must continue moving, even if it means a running fight. We cannot expect to be successfully extracted from the claws of a dug-in enemy unit. The cool of morning surrenders to the heat of day and we continue to the east; we have re-entered Vietnam. Now more than ever I realize that the border is merely a line on a piece of paper; it means nothing.

Our movement is downhill until we have reached the bottom of a shallow ravine; now we return to the familiar uphill struggle. The team has not eaten today, there is no time to stop; we have to distance ourselves from the enemy above. The radio operator has reported to the relay that a concentration of enemy, probably a base camp, is dug in along the west end of the ridgeline. We will not ask for an AO, we will wait; with the arrival of the little observer aircraft, the enemy will know a recon team is nearby and will begin to search for it. It is best to continue moving and to stay out of the deep ravines in order to maintain radio contact; we cannot afford intermittent transmissions in such a hostile area.

Late afternoon is turning to dusk; moving with extreme stealth has slowed our progress to barely a full kilometer through the thick jungle since we heard the rooster crow. It is time to search for a defendable harbor site; dark will be on us soon. We move up onto a small, steep-sided hill that straddles the border. There are two huge trees that have fallen one on top of the other and after so much time they seem to have merged into one mass of decaying pulp. From their trunks grow bright green ferns and brown mushrooms; huge black scorpions watch from under the shedding bark … waiting for the dark. We will stay hidden here throughout the night. Behind us looms the mountain that we abandoned; I pray that they have not observed our movement. It is doubtful that we are capable of defending this little rise against a force that is large enough to utilize field phones and keep chickens. The Claymores are set in a triangle pattern; their blasts and back-blasts will hopefully overlap, creating an unavoidable killing zone. I ask for an extraction the following morning; we wait for the answer, night is once again upon us.

In the dark, unable to see, we open cans of rations and wolf down the contents. Unable to read the labels in the dark; we only know what we are eating by the taste and smell. I have opened a can of "Beefsteak and Potatoes," a meal that I usually throw away. But for some reason the chunks of fat laden, salted beef taste delicious. Even the potatoes that are crammed into the cans half-cooked seem edible. I wonder if not looking at the grease-caked contents of the green cans makes the food more appetizing. Each man digs a small hole with his Ka-Bar and buries the cans; we do not want to leave a trail for the enemy to follow. There is no word on the extraction. Before dark, I located a nice LZ perhaps four hundred meters below and to the north of the harbor site. The position has been coded with the shackle sheet and will be given when the relay calls for it. The night is long and everyone remains awake; there has been very little sleep since our insertion.

Midnight arrives and approximately fifteen hundred meters to the north we see a string of small, blinking lights moving through our RZ. The enemy is moving to the northwest; they often use the tiny perfume bottle oil lamps to maintain the integrity of a supply column. The radio operator and I crawl under a poncho with the map and a penlight. From the map we determine that the column is moving along a stream that flows from Nui Giang Gio northwest to the middle of our RZ and then due north to the Da Krong River. The stream empties into the river within one kilometer of where we were shot down in ET-3. This must be a part of the same trail that we were sent to locate for the General. With no artillery support, we helplessly watch as the tiny blinking lights move along the predetermined route. We are advised that there will be an observer aircraft overhead at first light; he will locate the enemy and send air strikes against them. To our northeast, one of the Stingray teams has also observed a separate column of dim lights that are also moving along the floor of the Da Krong Valley; it is a busy night for everyone.

Before daylight we are advised that our extraction will go at 0800. We give the coded LZ position to the relay and prepare to move. The Claymores are collected and our team begins to move through the dark, down the hill toward the LZ that is located where the canopy gives way to the vast expanse of high elephant grass that fills the valley. To the east the sky once again begins to turn pale; there is no time to waste, we must be in place for the extraction before the AO arrives. As the sun begins to rise over the Annam Cordillera, we have reached a position very near the LZ that we have picked. We are well hidden in the high grass; the dark has concealed our movement from the searching eyes of the observers and mortar crews. Fear is with us; he has decided to wait with our team in the sea of green grass. I push him away but he is determined to stay with me. As the rising sun burns into the dew-drenched valley, we take turns searching along the stream with the field glasses; the radio is silent. The extraction must occur as soon as possible; we cannot stay in any one place for very long. The AO has arrived and is circling above as we give the position of the column of lights; his arrival has announced our presence. The enemy will search for us now; he will send patrols down from the camp above, searching for our trail that will be so easy to locate. It is 0800; there are no helicopters, I consider moving back into the dark safety of the canopy. The radio operator whispers that the helicopters are enroute; soon we hear the familiar popping of CH-46 engines coming from the northwest. The radio is in contact with the lead gun ship. The operator advises them of the confirmed enemy positions to the north and south, and of the probable enemy observers to the east. High above we hear the high pitched roar of jet engines as the Phantoms circle on station waiting for the command to blast the valley or assist in our extraction. Huey gun ships suddenly appear, crossing the LZ with lightning speed. Both gun ships turn abruptly and fire rockets back toward our position. The rockets cross directly above us and explode along the sloping approaches to Hill 765 and the enemy camp. The aerial observer is working along the stream, searching for the enemy unit that moved along it during the night. Suddenly, perhaps from five hundred meters to the north, a stream of white-purple 12.7mm tracers passes by the tiny single engine plane; the grenadier points to the stream of flaming pearls and calmly whispers, "twelve sevens," and each of the team nods in agreement. The pilot seems to pay no attention to the heavy machine guns; he rolls back in and fires a white phosphorous rocket at the enemy gun emplacement. As we are watching the fearless observer crew, the troop ships suddenly appear. The lead ship wants a yellow smoke to identify our team; it is immediately popped and tossed into the grass. He begins his run into the LZ; I give the boarding order, but realize that I am only talking to myself. The boarding order is a complete waste of time because the team will get aboard any way it can. No one will be left behind, that is all that matters, everyone will get aboard. The helicopter approaches and I am face to face with the two pilots that seem so vulnerable behind the thin, transparent plastic. Like a restless stallion, the lurching machine is held in a hover as it swaps ends; the open ramp is only thirty feet from us. We struggle through the grass; the starboard gunner suddenly unleashes a volley from his fifty-caliber Browning at possible enemy positions, the machine gun fire immediately erupts from the port gun as well. The gun-ships make rocket and machine gun runs along the ridgeline behind us. Our team wades through the matted grass that traps each leg and foot; bent forward, we struggle into the typhoon winds of the rotor wash. The radio operator falls and we drag him; in the deafening engine noise, enemy gunfire is seldom heard, I pray that the radioman has merely slipped and fallen. We reach the gaping cargo ramp and the first man climbs on and turns to help the rest of us; I am relieved that the radio operator has climbed aboard with no assistance. The helicopter seems dark inside and the gunners, wearing helmets, their faces hidden behind tinted visors, resemble huge insects. I push everyone forward into the cavernous interior of the still hovering chopper; seeing that the other three men are still in front of me, I wave to the gunners who advise the pilot that we are aboard. It has only taken a brief second; we are climbing fast, the gunners continue to fire into the grass below. Looking through the window I see a wall of yellow-orange napalm, trailing a cloud of black oily smoke, roll along the stream; we gain altitude while circling, below the stream turns into a caldron.

The wind howls through the helicopter and chills our sweat-soaked uniforms. Exhausted, I stretch out on the nylon seat and close my eyes ... sleep comes fast.

16

Home

The man was right; you can never go home, especially to something that no longer exists, and probably never did. Perhaps home is merely an imagined haven, a special place where the ravaged mind may travel to seek solace. Maybe it is not a place at all, but rather a dream-driven fantasy that is filled with Norman Rockwell illustrations; possibly an illusion that creates a gripping nostalgia by supplying vivid, holly-berry framed visions of happy homespun charm. The delusion assumes the reality of a cozy sweet-smelling kitchen, where a plump, cheery, apron-clad mother removes steaming hot apple pies from a warm, toasty oven at Christmas time. Or ... was home the leech-infested mountains we prowled with those that became our family?

I return to America in December 1968, having spent exactly twenty months and twenty days in Quang Tri Province. In the early spring of 1969, after being passed from clinic to clinic where my re-emerging malaria is dealt with and without being asked to re-enlist; I am decorated, processed, and quickly returned to the life that I abandoned four years earlier. Like so many others, I immediately seek refuge within a thick shell and allow no one to penetrate; I repel all advances while maintaining the integrity of the perimeter ... always defending ... always scanning ... always eluding. America, engrossed in self-flagellation, is foundering in a sea of turmoil; I am a stranger in a strange land. Successfully, I find escape and solace in the depths of seclusion and hard work; I seldom emerge.

Seeking anonymity, I bury myself deep within the arduous isolation of a fisherman's life. The heritage that I once attempted to escape and abandon has now become my refuge. I never permit my mind to dwell on the events of the past and yet, although the bittersweet memories of the Truong Son are purged from my mind and sent into the depths of a dark abyss, each day they claw their way to the surface and remain just long enough to generate the gut-wrenching spasms conjured by anger and frustration. For many years, home is merely a "harbor site" established within one of the generic apartments that seem to always surround a remote and obscure marina; while the palm fronds rustle in the wind and with a locked and loaded Colt A-1 within arm's reach, my mind drifts into a vibrant world of vivid dreams that I will one day realize are actually terror-filled nightmares. Hours before the sun rises I am once again steering the boat through the maze of red and green lights that lead to the deep cobalt blue of the Gulf Stream; long after the sun has crossed the sky, I will return to the island by steering the fish-laden vessel through these same markers. Another day passes, and I remain poised along the outer perimeter of society; happily, I assume the role of observer rather than participant. Totally independent, I become the essence of capitalism; America owes me nothing and I have asked for nothing. I am content to live within the parameters of the idyllic lifestyle that I have been blessed with and merely want to be left alone; I am thankful to be alive.

It was in a Key West café one evening, while enjoying a plate of *picadillo* that suddenly, I lost faith in my country. As my eyes strained at the snowy intermittent pictures that escaped an old black and white television set, I watched in silent bewilderment as we abandoned our South Vietnamese allies. The mangled legs hanging from the wheel wells of transport planes seemed the fitting termination to a conflict long controlled by the egomaniacal politicians that prevented victory. As I watched Saigon fall, whispered, venom-filled curses escaped my lips; just as America had abandoned brave freedom fighters on the bloodstained beaches that fringe the Bay of Pigs, she has betrayed another friend. Memories of hunger and thirst cross my mind; the faces of dear friends wrapped in filthy ponchos summon waves of frustration and anxiety. With my stomach twisted into tight knots, I am unable to finish my dinner. My eyes scan the crowded café; there is no concern, no one watches the fading picture nor shares my torment ... I have never felt so alone. As I step into the balmy night air, the warm, freshening breeze blowing from Cuba clears the faces from my mind and loosens the tight knots that constrict my stomach; I wander aimlessly and alone into the sleepless tropical night. When the day returns I will again prowl the northern edge of the Gulf Stream; beneath a blistering sun that reflects from the blue-silver mirrored sea, I will toil within a sweat-soaked trance until the lingering confusion is mercifully purged from my mind.

With marriage comes a softening of the protective shell and with the passing of time, the "harbor site" becomes a home or perhaps ... a "bunker." I remain an outsider in a land that I seldom understand and though I am a Vietnam Veteran, I am unable to relate to the camouflage-clad, drug-ridden, homeless horde that has come to represent our generation of warrior. Along the wall of black stone that is embedded with familiar names that conjure nightmare visions; an army of these "killer-elite" icons hustle for spare change, most are too young to have known the horror. Nearby, souvenir stands provide a carnival-like ambiance while soft, pudgy, middle-aged "professional veterans," adorned in vast assortments of berets, medallions, patches, and boots, talk openly of clandestine insertions into the very lair of an enemy fashioned by myth; and though they have spent endless hours in preparation, the fantasy that they hope to project remains incomplete ... they lack the eyes that reflect predation, fear, thirst and hunger.

In time, those that do possess scanning wolf eyes will again seek the camaraderie that was once shared among brothers in a far off despondent land. Like lost children, we will wander cautiously back into the fold of a family that traverses a wide spectrum of mainstream America—firefighters, doctors, teachers, police officers, filmmakers, bankers, social workers, mechanics, politicians, merchants, attorneys, construction workers, fishermen, farmers, salesmen, career Marines, athletic coaches and men of the cloth; we hardly bear a resemblance to the stereotype. A code of honor forged long ago beneath the canopy of the Truong Son provides both the integrity and endurance needed to successfully navigate the path that twists through life. Each individual is a link that bonds the family circle and each is as important as the next; no one will be left behind.

Conclusion

As I complete this work, I suddenly realize that I have passed through a circle of time and space that now ends where it began. From my hotel window I look west, toward the lair of my protector and the ancient jagged green mountain grottos that are beginning to absorb the setting sun; recollections of past sunsets fill my mind. Though apprehensive, I no longer fear the coming black void; yet vivid memories, left by an icy-fingered companion, still linger somewhere in the subliminal depths of my subconscious mind. I am attached to this land and these people by an adhesion that I am unable to fully comprehend; I do not attempt to search for an answer but instead, I accept and do not question, perhaps ... I am home.

The soothing dusk approaches and my balcony is set ablaze by a firestorm of brilliant colors; I immerse myself into the shimmering spectacle. As the last stubborn ray of light is reluctantly absorbed into the black of the Annam Cordillera, my mind is drawn to those ragged, skinny, teenaged warriors that fought so tenaciously defending two borders of a ravaged, desperate land; yes, these were and will always be my true family, my comrades, my peers ... my brothers. To them I say ... Semper Fi.

John Edmund Delezen
Hue, Vietnam
September 2001

In Memoriam

Oh! Brothers; our trail was long lay'd,
Toward eastern sonnets singing of ancient crystal'd jade,
West, across the endless bounds of sapphire flow,
Where time is scented jasmine and fate colored sloe.

Through era and epoch, piercing history past,
Testing the fury of the beast with shaded faith made fast,
And on, across shadowed chasms that terror once creased,
But alas … we were born in the west to die in the east.

Oh! Brothers; behold the ancestral path,
Following ribbon'd flame beneath the raptors wrath,
South, along the verdant spine of our mother's breast,
Traversing the beloved realm that time has caress'd.

Credulous youth is summon'd by angel'd voices that dare,
While moldering squander'd ivory, send cries of c'est la guerre,
And on, riding the tiger from the dragon's blazing mouth,
But alas … we were born in the north to die in the south.

Ted Bishop	*Dennis Christie*	*James M. Fuhrman*
Michael A. Bodamer	*Jimmy L. Craig*	*Arthur Garcia*
David E. Boyer	*Nevitt Davis*	*Henry Granillo*
Robert J. Bridges	*Stephen Emrich*	*Terrance Graves*
John R. Cabrini	*John D. Flanagan*	*Bruce Gruenwald*
Adam Cantu	*John J. Foley III*	*Michael Havranek*
Charles D. Chomel	*Roy Fryman*	*James E. Honeycutt*

In Memoriam

Curtis W. Hurlock
Allen Hutchinson
Henry Imes
Charles Johnson
Martin Keefe
Freddie Ray Kelley
John Killen
James W. Kooi
Lawrence Leigh, Jr.
Lawrence G. Leise

Adrien S. Lopez
Ronald W. McLean
Andrew Marcotte
Chester Mollett
Robert Moore
James Moshier
Carl Myllymaki
Nicholas Natzke
William Nelms
Douglas O'Donnell

Robert Rohweller
Carlos A. Rosa
Jose Rosas
Daniel Savage
Michael Scanlon
Dillon Tate
James Thompson
Robert Thompson
Alexander Ward
James Widener

...Our fallen brothers

Glossary

AK   7.62mm Chinese type 56 or Soviet AK-47 assault rifle

AO   Arial Observer; the AO flew in the backseat of an unarmed single engine O1 Cessna Bird Dog. He directed close air support, while the pilot flew the aircraft and marked targets with white phosphorous rockets; the Bird Dog replaced by the twin engine O2A Cessna.

ATL   assistant team leader

C-4   a plastic explosive

CH-34   old but reliable single-rotor helicopter, replaced by the CH-46

CH-46   twin rotor, medium lift helicopter, affectionately called "frogs" by their crews

CH-53   heavy lift helicopter, often called the "Jolly Green Giant"

Claymore   directional anti-personnel mine

Colt A-1   a .45-caliber semi-automatic pistol, Colt 1911 A-1

DMZ   demilitarized zone, a buffer area dividing North and South Vietnam, often called the "Dead Marine Zone"

Flechette   steel darts

Grenadier   Marine assigned to carry M-79 grenade launcher

Grid square   one square kilometer

Grunt   a name given to Marine ground troops by aviators during the Korean War. During the Vietnam War, the U.S. Army adopted the term as well.

Glossary

Gunny   Gunnery Sergeant, E-7

Gunship   UH-1 "Huey" helicopter heavily armed with rockets and machine guns

Harbor site   night position

Hooch or hootch   living quarters, most often a tropical hut, approximately 20 feet by 40 feet, tin roofed with screen sides

Ka-Bar   Marine Corps utility-fighting knife

Klick   one kilometer

LZ   helicopter landing zone, most often the slope of a steep mountain

M-14   a 7.62mm rifle used by the Marines until 1967; the M-16 rifle replaced the reliable weapon

M-16   a 5.56mm controversial American assault rifle

M-60   a 7.62mm general purpose machine gun

M-79   a single shot grenade launcher that fired a 40mm round

Northern I Corps   northern edge of the most northern tactical area of South Vietnam

Nuoc mam   fermented fish sauce, a Southeast Asia staple

Nuoc mia   sugar cane juice with lime added

On call   defensive artillery concentrations plotted before dark

R&R   rest and relaxation, respite from battle

RZ   reconnaissance zone or recon zone, an area to patrol to gather information about the enemy, often an area covering six grid squares

Sit-reps   situation reports, sent by radio

SKS Carbine   7.62mm Soviet-Chinese semiautomatic rifle, most often issued to support troops

"Spooky," AKA "Puff the Magic Dragon"   a U.S. Air Force C-47 cargo plane converted into an extremely lethal gunship armed with fast firing 7.62mm "mini-guns"

Tra xanh   green tea; often contains medicinal properties

"Twelve Sevens"   12.7mm Soviet heavy machine gun

Index

Index

Index

Index